Volume I

QUICK & EASY
CHRISTMAS
CRAFTS

133 projects for gifts, ornaments and holiday decorating

The publishers and designers wish to thank the following companies for providing materials used in this publication:
- **Adhesive Technologies, Inc.** for low temperature glue guns and sticks
- **Aldastar Corp.** for pom poms
- **Aleene's** for tacky craft glue, fabric glue and fabric stiffener
- **All Cooped Up Designs** for curly crepe wool doll hair
- **Artifacts, Inc.** for tassels
- **Binney & Smith** for air-dry clay
- **Carnival Arts, Inc.** for spray paints, spray glitter, spray webbing, spray adhesive and graining tool
- **C. M. Offray & Son, Inc.** for ribbons
- **Creative Beginnings** for brass charms
- **D & CC** for papier-mâché boxes
- **DecoArt** for acrylic paints
- **Delta Technical Coatings, Inc.** for acrylic paints, dimensional paints, sealers and varnishes
- **Flora Craft** for Styrofoam® and floral foams
- **Forster, Inc.** for wood turnings
- **Jesse M. James & Co.** for buttons
- **Libbey, Inc.** for apothecary jars
- **Lion Ribbon Company** for ribbons
- **MPR Associates Inc.** for twisted paper ribbon
- **Novtex Corp.** for braids and trims
- **One & Only Creations** for curly doll hair
- **Peking Handicrafts, Inc.** for doilies
- **Plaid Enterprises, Inc.** for dimensional fabric paint
- **Spice Market, Inc.** for potpourri and cinnamon sticks
- **St. Louis Trimming Inc.** for lace and self-adhesive trims
- **Sweet Antiques Inc.** for the square spice bottle and pyramid bottle
- **Wang's International Inc.** for jingle bells, garlands, baskets, silk flowers and teddy bears
- **Wimpole Street** for doilies

Styrofoam® is a registered trademark of Dow Chemical Corporation.
Fimo® is a registered trademark of Eberhard Faber GmBH, EFA-Str. 1, 92318 Neumarkt/Germany.

Oxmoor House
Editor-in-Chief: Nancy Fitzpatrick Wyatt
Senior Crafts Editor: Susan Ramey Cleveland
Senior Editor, Editorial Services: Olivia K. Wells
Art Director: James Boone

Hot Off The Press
Project Editor: Mary Margaret Hite
Technical Editor: LeNae Gerig
Photographer: Meredith Marsh
Graphic Designer: Sally Clarke
Digital Imagers: Shawn Jarvey
      Michael Kincaid
      Larry Seith
Editors: Paulette McCord Jarvey
      Teresa Nelson
      Tom Muir

published by

in association with **Oxmoor House®**

and **LEISURE ARTS® CRAFT LEAFLETS**

Library of Congress Catalog Card Number 96-69844
Hardcover ISBN 0-8487-1560-8
Softcover ISBN 0-8487-1564-0

Printed in the United States of America
First printing 1996

Volume I

QUICK & EASY
CHRISTMAS
CRAFTS

133 projects for gifts,
ornaments and holiday
decorating

Table of Contents

Decorate & Celebrate

A Collection of Santas

An Armful of Angels

Quick & Easy Gifts

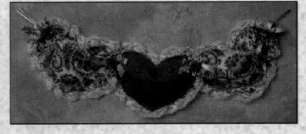

BUY IT & EMBELLISH IT!

Frosty Friendlies

TREE TREASURES

Hints, Tips & Techniques

Decorate & Celebrate

Decorating your home for Christmas inspires special feelings that last through the holiday season and turn into fond memories. Wreaths, candles and baskets, all dressed up with ribbons, silk flowers, pine and fir boughs, spread warmth and cheer through every room.

This section includes designs for whimsical decorating featuring teddy bears and plush reindeer. For elegant Christmas decorations, we've included such items as gorgeous candles and a wreath decorated with mauve and gold. If your taste runs toward a country Christmas, there is a painted terra cotta pot to hold candy or a personalized mailbox filled with pine sprigs.

There's even a beautifully decorated and useful basket to hold Christmas cards. Or, if you need an unusual gift, fill the basket with homemade goodies or articles for a special evening by a cozy fireplace. No doubt the lucky recipient of either gift will greatly enjoy it.

To coordinate one look throughout your home, substitute similar flowers or materials for the ones listed in these projects. Turn the Reindeer Card Holder into a country piece by replacing the reindeer with a cluster of red silk roses, then adding baby's breath throughout the pine sprigs.

Here's another quick and easy decorating idea—pine garlands are a great investment! They can be cut into shorter pieces and used as swags to place on windowsills, over mirrors or as quick centerpieces. Just add a few silk flowers, some holly and trail a ribbon through the length of the swag—it's perfect!

Whatever your decorating theme, all the pieces in this section are sure to enhance and beautify your home, providing hours of enjoyment during the holidays.

Poinsettia Swag
by Teresa Nelson & LeNae Gerig

2 stems of white/gold silk poinsettias, each with one 5" and one 7" wide blossom, one 1½" wide burgundy apple, a 1" wide yellow apple, three ¾"–1" wide burgundy raspberries, two ⅜"–1" wide burgundy cherries, one ¾" wide peach pomegranate and many 3"–4½" long leaves
one 20" wide vine arch
4 dusty green vinyl spruce branches, each with twelve 4"–5" sprigs
24-gauge wire, low temperature glue gun and sticks or tacky craft glue
1 ½ yards of 2¾" wide metallic gold mesh wired ribbon
1 ⅝ yards of ⅝" wide metallic gold/cream satin cord

1 Cut each poinsettia stem to 20". Wire to the arch with the stems overlapping and the tips extending 6" past the ends of the arch.

2 Cut each pine stem into four 3-sprig sections. Glue them evenly spaced among the poinsettias.

3 Loop and glue mesh ribbon through the swag from one end to the other.

4 Use the cord to make a loopy bow (see page 140) with two 3½" and two 5" loops, a 13" tail and a 15" tail. Knot the cord ends. Glue the bow to the center of the swag as shown in the large photo. Make a wire hanger (see page 144) at the top back.

Evergreen Wreath
by Teresa Nelson & LeNae Gerig

one 20" wide green vinyl pine wreath
2⅔ yards of 2¾" wide gold/mauve lamé wire-edged ribbon
4 rose/cone picks, each with one 2½" wide peach rose, two 1½" mauve roses, one 2" long gold
*   cone, three ¾" wide gold berries, three 2" long pine sprigs and many 1½"–2½" long leaves*
one 9" tall ivy bush with nine 4"–6" branches of ¾"–2" wide leaves
three 2¼" wide mauve jingle bells, gold acrylic paint, #2 flat paintbrush
paper towels, low temperature glue gun and sticks or tacky craft glue

1 Use the ribbon to make a puffy bow (see page 141) with a center loop and six 3" loops, a 15" tail and a 25" tail. Glue to the upper left of the wreath. Loop and glue the 15" tail over the top and the 25" tail down the left side.

2 Dip the brush into the paint, then dab off most of the paint onto paper towels. Lightly brush the sides of the jingle bells, letting the mauve show through. Let dry; glue to the wreath as shown in the large photo.

3 From each pick cut a sprig containing the peach rose, two pine sprigs and leaves, leaving a second sprig with all the other components. Glue a peach rose sprig left of the bow and the remaining sprigs evenly spaced around the wreath, alternating types as shown.

4 Cut the ivy branches off the bush. Glue four around the bow as shown. Glue the rest evenly spaced throughout the wreath as shown in the large photo. Make a wire hanger at the upper back.

Fruit Swag
by Teresa Nelson

9' green vinyl pine garland
3 yards of 2¾" wide burgundy/green/black wire-edged
  tapestry ribbon
2¾ yards of ¼" wide burgundy cord
1 stem of latex pears with four 1½"–2" green pears and 5
  sprigs of three 2½"–3" leaves
3 apple/pine/cone picks, each with a 1½" burgundy apple, a
  2" cone, three ¾" green/burgundy blueberries, 3 pine
  sprigs, a cluster of pods, holly leaves and berries
2 burgundy artificial grape picks, each with a 5" cluster of ⅝"
  metallic grapes
six 40" stems of dried kiwi vine
24-gauge wire, wire cutters
low temperature glue gun and sticks or tacky craft glue

1 Cut a 31" and two 25" garland lengths. Place a 25" length on each side of the 31" length, tops even. Wire together 11" from the top, twisting the wire ends into a loop hanger at the back. Fluff the sprigs. Cut a kiwi vine to 29" and wire it to the swag center with the stem ends extending above the wired area. Repeat with a 23" kiwi on each side.

2 Use the ribbon to make an oblong bow (see page 140) with a 4" center loop, two 4½" and two 6" loops, an 18" and a 27" tail. Glue it over the wired area of the swag. Loop and tuck a tail down each side of the swag. Use the cord to make a loopy bow with six 3¾" loops, a 26" and a 21" tail. Glue it above the oblong bow, looping the tails down through the swag center.

3 Cut the apple pick stems to 3"; glue one above the bow, extending upward. Cut a 2" pear from the center of the stem and a 3-leaf sprig off the lower stem; glue these above and right of the pick. Cut the rest of the pear stem to 23" and wire over the swag center, extending downward. Glue an apple pick below left of the top pear on this stem and one below right of the second pear.

4 Glue one grape pick below the bow, curving downward. Glue the other below the last apple pick, curving under the lowest pear. Cut two 7" curly sections of kiwi and glue above the bows. Cut the remaining kiwi into 10"–18" sprigs; glue among the lower pine and fruit.

Decorated Basket

by Teresa Nelson

side view

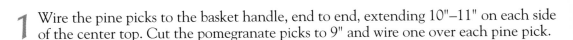

14"x11"x6"
vine basket with
an 8" tall handle
2⅔ yards of 2¾"
wide green/gold
lamé ribbon
2 gold-brushed vinyl
pine picks, each
with two 2"–3½"
cones and four 4"
pine sprigs
2 latex pomegranate
picks, each with a
1½" and two 2"
pomegranates and
6 grape leaves
2 Christmas picks,
each with 3 green pine sprigs, a gold ball, gold apple, 3 gold holly leaves, 14
berries and a gold bow
3 frosted gold berry picks, each with a 7" section of berries and a ¾" pine cone
1 oz. of green preserved princess pine, ½ oz. of preserved reindeer moss
30-gauge wire, low temperature glue gun and sticks or tacky craft glue

1 Wire the pine picks to the basket handle, end to end, extending 10"–11" on each side of the center top. Cut the pomegranate picks to 9" and wire one over each pine pick.

2 Cut the Christmas pick stems to 2"; wire one over each pomegranate pick. Cut a berry pick to 8" and wire to extend from below a pine pick to the handle base; repeat with the other pick on the other side.

3 Use the ribbon to make an oblong bow (see page 140) with a 3" center loop, six 4"–4¼" loops and 18" tails. Glue the bow angling across the handle top. Bring a tail down on each side of the handle and glue at the base as shown in the large photo. Glue a ¾" moss tuft over the glued area.

4 Cut the remaining berry pick into four 2"–4" sprigs. Glue a 2" sprig on each side of the bow and a 4" sprig on each side between the Christmas and pomegranate picks. Cut the princess pine into 3" sprigs; glue moss tufts and pine sprigs evenly spaced throughout the design, filling any empty spaces.

Teddy Bear Basket

by Teresa Nelson & LeNae Gerig

tan plush bears: one 12", one 10" tall
20"x5" round willow basket
7' green vinyl fir garland
4½ yards of 2⅝" wide red plaid taffeta
    wire-edged ribbon
3⅓ yards of ⅝" wide red satin ribbon
5 Christmas picks, each with a 1¼"
    wide gold drum, a 1" package, three
    ⅞" wide red balls, five ¼" red
    berries, three 3" long holly leaves and
    3" long pine sprigs
6 raspberry/berry picks, each with three
    1¼" long raspberries, ten ⅜" wide
    red berries and six 2"–3" long leaves
six 5½" long candy canes
1 oz. of bleached dried baby's breath
24-gauge wire
low temperature glue gun and sticks or
    tacky craft glue

1 (The basket will hang with its bottom against the wall.) Attach a 6" wire length to the upper back for a hanger. Cut an 18" garland length, bend it into a V and glue it inside the basket bottom extending upward. Wire the remaining garland around the basket rim.

2 Use four yards of plaid ribbon to make a puffy bow (see page 141) with a center loop, eight 4" loops, a 25" tail and a 35" tail. Glue to the upper left. Loop and glue the 25" tail over the top and the 35" tail down the left side to the center bottom. For the 12" bear's collar, pull one wire to gather one side of the remaining ribbon to 9". Wrap around the bear's neck and twist the wire ends at the back. Use 12" of satin ribbon to tie a shoestring bow with 1" loops and 2½" tails. Glue under his chin. Tie 18" of satin ribbon around the other bear's neck in a shoestring bow like the first. Glue the bears into the basket as shown.

3 Tuck and glue one end of the remaining satin ribbon behind the bow; loop and glue it around the basket front. Cut the Christmas pick stems to 2" long and glue them evenly spaced among the fir sprigs.

4 Cut the stem of each berry pick to 1½" and glue one on each side of the bow. Glue the rest evenly spaced among the Christmas picks. Glue a candy cane in the 12" bear's hand, one to the bow, and the rest evenly spaced around the wreath. Cut the baby's breath into 2"–3" sprigs and glue among the other materials as shown in the large photo.

Bear on a Ladder

by Teresa Nelson

24"x13" TWIGS™ ladder
12" tall burlap teddy bear
3 yards of 1½" wide cream burlap ribbon
18" of ¾" wide red/green/gold plaid ribbon
1 stem of green vinyl Canadian pine with
   3 branches of 6–8 sprigs
1 stem of green lacquered holly with 5 sprigs of 2½"–4"
   leaves, berries and twigs
3 apple picks, each with a 1" apple, 2 apple quarters and
   6 holly leaves
3 frosted red berry picks, each with ten ⅜"–½" berries,
   a ¾" cone and wired curls
24-gauge wire
low temperature glue gun and sticks or tacky craft glue

1 Wire the bear to sit on the second rung from the ladder bottom. Wrap the plaid ribbon around his neck and tie in a shoestring bow (see page 141) with 1½" loops and 5" tails. Cut three holly leaves and an apple off an apple pick and a small berry off the berry pick. Glue two leaves and the berry in the bow center. Glue the apple and remaining leaf in the bear's paw.

2 Cut the 8-sprig branch off the pine; spread the sprigs apart, cut the stem to 1" and glue to the upper left of the ladder. Cut the stems of the two 6-sprig branches to 1". Glue to the lower right corner, one extending left and one upward. Cut the cream ribbon in half. Use each half to make a puffy bow with a center loop, four 3" loops and one 23" tail. Glue one over the pine stems in the upper left corner, the other at the lower right. Loop the tails over the rungs as shown in the large photo.

3 Cut the holly stem into five sprigs. Glue two to the upper area, one extending down and one to the right. Glue two in the lower area, one extending upward and one left. Glue the last above the lower bow, angled toward the bear.

4 Cut the apple pick stems to 1". Glue the partial pick to the lower area, angled left. Glue a pick above the lower bow and one below the upper bow. Cut the stems of two berry picks to ½" and glue into the lower area, one extending upward and one left. Cut the last berry pick into two sprigs; glue into the upper area with one extending right and one down. Attach a wire loop hanger to the ladder back.

Pine Cone Basket

by Reva McCord

Note: Using floral foam to fill the basket makes this project so much faster to do—and also saves on pine cones!

14"x12"x4" willow basket with a 10" tall handle
2 yards of 1½" wide red/green/gold striped ribbon
sixteen 4"–5" long pine cones
10 stems of red artificial berries, each with 2 sprigs of many
   ¼" wide berries, 1½" long leaves and tendrils
two 3"x4"x8" blocks of floral foam for silks and drieds
6 stems of frosted green artificial pine, each with seven 3" long
   sprigs
4 oz. of sphagnum moss
gloss acrylic spray sealer, gold glitter spray
U-shaped floral pins, 22-gauge wire, wire cutters
low temperature glue gun and sticks or tacky craft glue

1 Glue one end of the ribbon to one side of the basket, inside the handle base. Wrap the ribbon spiral fashion around the handle, making the wraps 1½" apart. Trim excess and glue the other end. Use the remaining ribbon to make a puffy bow (see page 141) with a center loop, six 2½" loops and 5" tails. Glue to the outside basket rim next to the left handle base. Ripple and glue the tails as shown.

2 Cut the foam blocks in half lengthwise. Glue one piece into the center of the basket. Cut another piece as necessary, gluing it around the edges. Glue a third piece into the center, trimming if needed to keep the foam 2" below the rim. Cut and glue the last piece to fill any empty areas. Cover the foam with moss, securing it with U-pins.

3 Cut an 8" wire length, wrap around the lower petals of a pine cone and twist the ends. Cut the wire ends to 1½" long. Repeat for each cone. Dip the wire ends in glue and insert into the foam, placing each cone at a slightly different angle, to fill the basket. Spray the cones with gloss acrylic.

4 Cut the pine sprigs apart. Glue among the cones singly and in pairs. Cut the berry sprigs apart, leaving a 1" stem on each. Glue evenly spaced among the cones. Spray the cones and bow with glitter.

...and More Pine Cone Baskets

The two baskets shown above are overflowing with pine cones and greenery, providing a warm feeling whether displayed prominently on a hearth or tucked into a corner. Both were assembled as described for the basket on page 14, with varied materials.

To construct the smaller arrangement, begin by painting the basket green, then spraying gold glitter spray over it. This elegant look has been reinforced with smaller pine cones sprayed gold and tucked among the larger ones. To complete the look, small shoestring bows of gold lamé ribbon tie together clusters of gold berries and pods which are inserted among the cones. Finally, gold-edged plaid ribbon wraps the handle and is tied into a large, dressy bow, giving this basket a formal look.

The other arrangement began with a large basket which was roughly stained dark for a more rustic look. Golden touches were scattered throughout the arrangement, yet a country feeling was reinforced by including mixed greenery such as frosted pine, fir and holly. Adding to the informal look was the large shoestring bow made from printed ribbon— simple, yet elegant, giving this Christmas basket a country touch.

Gold Leaf Candle

by LeNae Gerig

Note: This candle is for decorative use only. Do not burn.

3"x6¼" red pillar candle
matte acrylic sealer
1" sponge brush
#8 flat shader paintbrush
gold leaf and gold leaf adhesive
4½"x1½" terra cotta saucer
acrylic paints: ivory, metallic gold
1" piece of household sponge
paper plate, paper towels
1 yard of ⅝" wide red/gold braid trim
low temperature glue gun and sticks or tacky craft glue

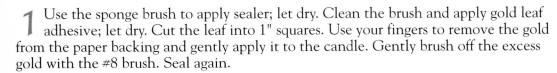

1 Use the sponge brush to apply sealer; let dry. Clean the brush and apply gold leaf adhesive; let dry. Cut the leaf into 1" squares. Use your fingers to remove the gold from the paper backing and gently apply it to the candle. Gently brush off the excess gold with the #8 brush. Seal again.

2 Seal the saucer; let dry. Paint it ivory, inside and out. Let dry, then pour a puddle of gold paint onto a paper plate. Dip the 1" sponge piece into the paint, dab off the excess on a paper towel, and sponge over the inside and outside of the saucer—don't cover it completely, but let some ivory show through. Let dry.

3 Glue trim around the top and bottom of the candle, and around the saucer rim. Place the candle in the saucer.

Sponged Star Candle

by LeNae Gerig

2¾"x9" white pillar candle
seven 2½" wide wooden stars
seven 1" wide wooden stars
metallic acrylic paints: gold, silver
3½" square of compressed sponge
gold spray webbing
matte acrylic spray sealer
paper plate, paper towels
#6 flat paintbrush
low temperature glue gun and sticks or tacky craft glue

1 Spray the candle with sealer; let dry. Spray with webbing; let dry.

2 Trace the large wooden star onto the compressed sponge; cut out. Repeat for the small star. Rinse the sponges with water to expand them; squeeze out excess moisture. Pour a small puddle of gold paint onto a paper plate. Dip the large sponge into the paint, blot excess paint on paper towels, and sponge four stars randomly spaced over the candle surface. Repeat to make four small gold stars.

3 Clean the sponges. Pour a small puddle of silver paint onto the plate and follow step 2 to sponge three large and five small silver stars among the gold ones. Let dry; spray with sealer.

4 Paint four large wooden stars and three small ones gold. Paint the remaining wooden stars silver. Glue the large stars around the candle base, alternating colors. Glue the small stars over the large ones as shown.

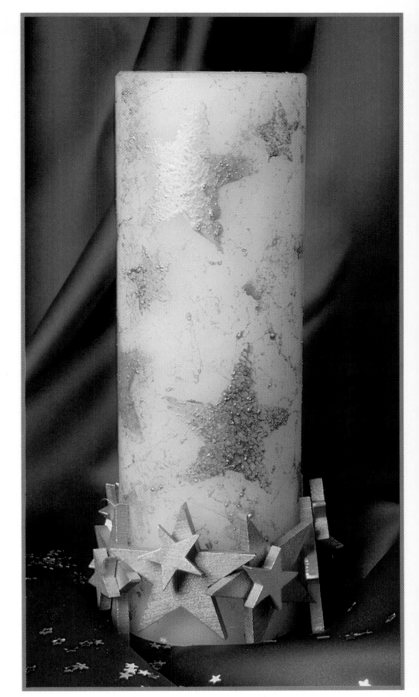

Note: This candle is for decorative use only. Do not burn.

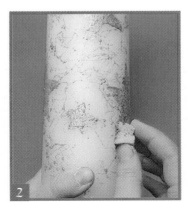

Potpourri Pot

by LeNae Gerig

3 ½"x4 ½" terra cotta pot
1 ½"x4 ½" terra cotta saucer
gold leaf, adhesive
acrylic paints: burgundy, dark green, metallic gold
flat paintbrushes: #10, #4
1" sponge paintbrush
old toothbrush
fine sandpaper, soft cloth
matte acrylic sealer
burgundy and gold potpourri
low temperature glue gun and sticks or tacky craft glue

1 Sand the pot and saucer to remove any rough edges. Wipe clean with a soft cloth. Use the sponge brush to apply sealer over all surfaces of the pot and saucer; let dry.

2 Clean the sponge brush and use it to paint the pot and saucer burgundy, inside and out—don't paint the rims. Let dry, then paint the rims green. Let dry.

3 Use the #10 brush to apply gold leaf adhesive to the rims. Let dry until clear. Gently tear off ¼"–1" pieces of gold leaf and apply with your fingertips, leaving small empty areas for the paint to show through. Use the #4 brush to remove any excess gold leaf.

4 Dip the toothbrush in gold paint, then rub your thumb across the bristles to spatter the pot and saucer with gold as shown in the large photo. Clean the #10 brush and use it to apply another coat of sealer. Set the pot in the saucer and fill with potpourri.

Mailbox with Cardinals

by Teresa Nelson

6 ½"x4 ½" red mailbox
two 3 ¾" long red fat cardinals
¼ oz. of white dried starflowers
small handful of Spanish moss
white acrylic paint
#0 round paintbrush
brown floral tape
4"x2"x2 ½" block of floral foam
    for silks, 2 U-shaped floral pins
tracing paper, transfer paper, pencil
1 stem of green vinyl pine with seven 4" sprigs
1 apple/cone pick with one 1 ½" wide red apple, ¾" wide burgundy berries, one 1 ½" wide pine
    cone, six ¾"–1" long mini cones, 3 pine sprigs, holly leaves and many ¼" wide red berries
low temperature glue gun and sticks or tacky craft glue

1 Open the mailbox. Paint a line of white stitching around the front, back and lower edge of the mailbox. Make a row of hearts (see the pattern at right) next to the front and back stitches, then make another row of stitches inside the hearts. Repeat on the rim of the door. Paint a line of stitches around the flag and a heart in the flag center. Dip the brush handle in white paint and touch to the surface to make three dots on each side of the heart. Transfer (see page 143) "THE" and the letters for your name below the flag. Go over the letters with white paint and decorate them with dots. Paint a heart and dots below your name.

2 Cut the foam to fit inside the mailbox and glue in place; cover with moss and secure with U-pins. Cut and set aside two pine sprigs for step 3. Cut the stem of the pine to 1" and glue into the foam. Cut four red berries and two mini cones off the pick and set aside for step 3. Cut the stem of the pick to 3" and glue into the center of the foam.

3 Curve the remaining pine sprigs into a natural shape and glue to the center top of the mailbox. Glue a bird to the center, then glue two berries and a cone on each side of the bird. Glue the remaining bird to the door arrangement as shown.

4 Hold five starflower stems together and floral tape (see page 144) 1" below the blossoms. Cut the stems to 3". Repeat for ten more clusters. Glue evenly spaced into the door arrangement. Repeat to make four 3-flower clusters, but tape these ½" below the blossoms and cut the stems to 1"; glue these around the upper bird as shown in the large photo.

THE
ABCDEFG
IJKLM
NOPQRS
UVWXYZ
ooo ♡ ooo

Gingerbread Christmas Pot

by Teri Stillwaugh

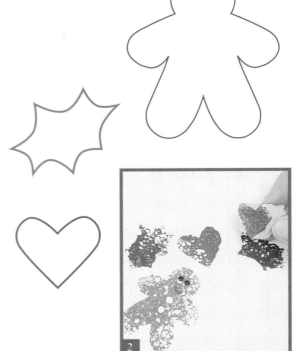

5¾" wide terra cotta pot
acrylic paints: ivory, metallic gold, tan, red, green, black, white
#10/0 liner brush, 1" sponge brush, old toothbrush
one 3"x5" sheet of compressed sponge
fine sandpaper, soft cloth or painter's tack cloth
tracing paper, pencil, paper plates, water-based acrylic sealer and varnish

1   Sand off any sharp edges of the pot; wipe clean with a cloth. Use a sponge brush to apply sealer all over the pot; let dry for 30 minutes. Clean the sponge brush and use it to paint the outside ivory. Paint the inside and bottom metallic gold; let dry. Pour gold paint onto a paper plate, dip in the toothbrush and rub your thumb over the bristles to spatter the outside of the pot.

2   Trace the patterns and cut from the sponge; soak in water, then squeeze out excess. Referring to the large photo, sponge five evenly spaced tan gingerbread boys over the pot. Sponge five red hearts between them. Sponge five sets of two green leaves. Sponge five red hearts between each set on the rim.

3   Dip the handle of the liner paintbrush in black, then touch to dot two eyes on each boy. Repeat with white for three buttons on each. Use the brush tip to paint red smiles.

4   Use the liner brush to add gold outlines and leaf veins. Let dry. Use the sponge brush to apply varnish in long, even strokes; let dry. **Note:** Because water will seep through and damage the paint, keep plants in a plastic container or use a plastic liner inside the painted pot.

Wall Basket Card Holder

by Teresa Nelson
& LeNae Gerig

12"x11½"x6½" wall basket
4' vinyl fir garland
3 yards of burgundy/green/gold tapestry ribbon
6 Christmas picks, each with five 2" long holly leaves, one 1"
   mauve package, one 1" wide burgundy apple, twelve ¼"
   burgundy berries and a 1" long pine spray
2 berry stems, each with seven 4" sprigs of three ⅝" burgundy
   berries
½ oz. of preserved rice grass
24-gauge wire, wire cutters
low temperature glue gun and sticks or tacky craft glue

1 Starting at the left side of the basket, wire the garland around the front rim and over the top of the basket. Curve the sprigs to extend right to left along the rim and left to right over the top.

2 Use the ribbon to make a puffy bow (see page 141) with a center loop, six 3" loops, a 24" tail and a 36" tail. Glue to the left of the basket. Loop the 24" tail over the top to the right side, gluing every 3"–4". Repeat with the 36" tail along the front rim.

3 Cut the stems of the picks to 1". Glue one above the bow, one below the bow and four evenly spaced among the fir sprigs.

4 Cut the sprigs off the berry stems and glue them evenly spaced throughout the garland, following the directions of the sprigs. Cut the rice grass into 3"–4" sprigs and glue evenly spaced as shown in the large photo.

of Santas

Santas aren't just for Christmas any more! They can be found peeking out from among collectibles in many houses these days. Whether it's an old-fashioned roly-poly Santa or a very staid and serious Father Christmas, when put together with a collection of favorite toys or antiques they add personality and animation to the grouping.

To create a "collection," pull all the pieces you want to display together in one area—a cabinet, shelf or mantel, for example. They don't have to be valuable, just special to you and some-how related to each other (all antiques, toys, tinware, glass-ware, etc.). Usually it looks best to place the largest or tallest piece near the center of the display space. Then work toward each end, placing the larger pieces near the back of the shelf.

Add smaller pieces among those already placed. At this point, it becomes an exercise of personal preference. Place the pieces you like best in prominent locations to draw attention to them. The pieces that aren't so important to you become the back-ground for your favorites. Be aware of the textures and colors of the pieces and mix them to add interest and pull the viewer's eye through the display.

You can add as many pieces as the shelf will hold, or make a couple of different groupings on one shelf. If placing two groups in close proximity, make one noticably smaller than the other. If you don't have enough "stuff," try adding in unusual pieces—sometimes the most surprising elements can make the whole collection come together.

These Santas work well among different antiques or reproduc-tions because they are placed in a pleasing arrangement, taking into consideration the size, color and texture differences. They relate to the collection because of their muted colors, nicely blending in among the older pieces. The Santas have added per-sonality to a collection that otherwise might have looked cold or sterile. And they can be left on display year-round!

actual height 5"

Santa Bell
by Cynthia Sullivan

one 3" wide (70mm) red jingle bell
4"x5" piece of red felt
one 1½" wide (35mm) wooden bead
¼ yard of ¼" wide black sequin trim
one ⅞" gold button
1 white bumpy chenille stem
one ¾" wide white pom pom
needle, 8" of gold metallic thread
white Mini Curl™ curly hair
pale peach acrylic paint, ¼" flat paintbrush
pink powdered blush, cotton swab
black fine-tip permanent pen
needlenose pliers, wire cutters
low temperature glue gun and sticks or tacky
   craft glue

Santa's hat

1 Use the pliers to twist the hanger off the bell top.
Paint the bead peach, let dry and glue for a head. Use
the pen to draw a nose and closed eyes. Blush the cheeks.
Glue the sequin trim for his belt. Cut the back off the
button and glue for a buckle.

2 Trace the hat pattern and cut from red felt. Glue the
straight edges together; let dry. For a hanger, thread
the needle with gold thread and take a stitch 1" above the
center front brim. Remove the needle and knot the
thread ½" from the ends. Glue the hat onto Santa's head.

3 Glue the bumpy chenille around the hat for a
brim—notice one bump is centered over Santa's
face. Glue the pom pom to the hat tip.

4 Pull the hat tip down on one side and glue the
pom pom to the brim. Cut the hair into 3"–4"
lengths. Fold each length in half and glue the fold to
the head, arranging the hair to form his beard and hair.

A Doll of a Santa

by Jackie Zars

one 3½" tall wooden pear
one 1¾" wide wooden ball knob
one ½" wide wooden button
1 flat wooden toothpick
acrylic paints: pale peach, coral, white, black
matte acrylic sealer
paintbrushes: #0 round, ½" flat
3" of 20-gauge gold wire
⅜ yard of ¼" wide ivory rope braid
½ pkg. of white Whimsey™ Hair
8½" of 18-gauge wire
one ½" wide ivory pom pom
3 green silk holly sprigs, each with
    four ½" long leaves and berries
one 1½" long frosted pine cone
needle, red thread
drill, ¹⁄₃₂" bit
tracing paper, transfer paper, pencil
low temperature glue gun and sticks or tacky craft glue

actual height 6½"

1 Head: Glue the button to the center front of the ball for a nose. Paint the head peach; let dry. Transfer (see page 143) the face pattern and paint as shown. Mix coral paint with an equal part of water to blush the cheeks. Let dry; seal.

2 Robe: Tear a 3½"x12" fabric strip. Sew a running stitch ¼" from one long edge, pull to gather and glue around the top of the wooden pear. Glue the back edges together. Glue 8" of braid to the robe front as shown.

3 Sleeves: Tear a 2"x8½" fabric strip. Place the 18-gauge wire in the center of the wrong side and fold the fabric in thirds over it. Glue to secure. Glue the center to the top back of the robe and bend the arms forward. Glue the cuffs together, then glue the pine cone to the center front. **Hood:** Cut a 6½"x3" fabric strip. Fold in half crosswise, right sides

together, and sew a ¼" seam from the fold to the lower edge. Turn right side out. Sew a running stitch along the lower edge (the one with the seam). Gather and glue to the body top as shown, leaving ½" unglued at each side front.

4 Glue the head to the body. Cut the hair into 10" lengths; fold each length into fourths. Glue one across the forehead and the others as shown to form the beard. Pull the hood up over the head, turn under a ½" hem and glue in place. Glue braid along the folded edge and the pom pom to the hat tip. Bend the gold wire around the paintbrush handle to form the glasses (see diagram); glue in place. Cut a 4-leaf holly sprig with berries and glue to the hat front as shown. Glue the remaining holly around the cone.

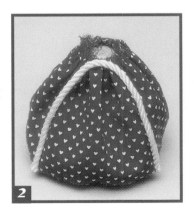

Egghead Santa

by Sallie Anderson

actual height 6"

one 2½" long plastic egg
1⅔ yards of white twisted paper ribbon
3" of red twisted paper ribbon
acrylic paints: pale peach, pink, black
matte acrylic sealer
paintbrushes: #12 flat, #2 round
one 1" wide white pom pom
4" of 24-gauge white cloth-covered wire
needle, 6" of gold thread
low temperature glue gun and sticks or tacky craft glue

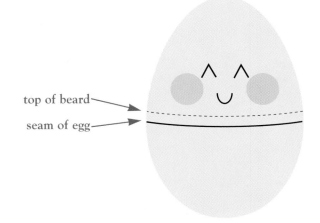

top of beard
seam of egg

1 Seal the egg, let dry, then paint it peach. Paint a black half-circle for the mouth and inverted V's for the eyes. Paint the cheeks peach. **Mustache:** Untwist a 1½" length of white paper ribbon and cut a 1½" square. Wrap cloth-covered wire tightly around the center and glue the mustache above the mouth.

2 Beard: Glue two 2" lengths of white twisted paper ribbon to the center front below the mouth. Repeat on each side of these lengths until the front of the egg is covered (this should take about 12 lengths). Trim the side lengths diagonally, gradually decreasing the lengths until the outside lengths measure 1¼" long. The lower edge of the beard should form a V.

3 Hair: Glue 1" lengths of white twisted paper ribbon around the back of his head—don't trim these.

4 Hat: Untwist the red paper ribbon and glue the sides together, forming a tube. Glue the bottom of the tube over his head. Pinch the top to a point and wire to secure. Glue the pom pom to the hat tip. **Hatband:** Cut a 7" length of white twisted paper ribbon and partially untwist to ½" wide. Glue around the lower edge of the hat. **Hanger:** Thread the needle with the gold thread and take a stitch through the hat top. Knot the ends together.

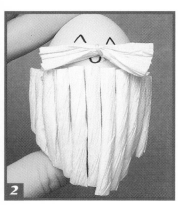

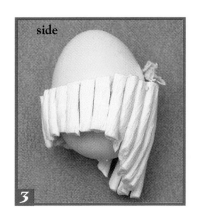

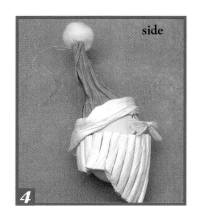

Twisted Paper Santa

by Nancy Overmyer

5" wide twisted paper ribbon:
20" of red, 8" of white
one 1½" wide Styrofoam® ball
2" square of long-napped white fur
¾"x5" of short-napped white fur
one ½" wide white pom pom
one ⅛" wide red pom pom
black acrylic paint
round wooden toothpick
20-gauge wire, wire cutters
low temperature glue gun and sticks
    or tacky craft glue

actual height 13"

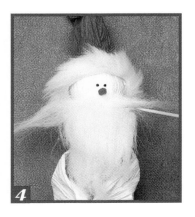

1 **Head:** Untwist the white paper ribbon. Place the foam ball 2" from one end and wrap the ribbon around it; glue the edges together. Twist both ends tightly close to the ball; wire to secure. Cut the paper ribbon in half from the center bottom almost to the neck and spread apart for arms.

2 **Body:** Untwist the red paper ribbon. Cut off 5" and set aside for the hat. Fold the remainder in half crosswise. Gather ½" from the ends, forming a ruffle, and insert the arms through the ruffle. Push the ruffle close to the head and wire tightly just below it. Bring the ends of the arms to the front and twist together 1" from the ends.

3 **Hat:** Glue the sides of the 5" red ribbon length together, forming a tube. Twist one end into a point and glue the other onto his head. Glue the white pom pom onto the point and the short-napped fur strip around the brim.

4 Glue the long-napped fur for his beard. Glue the red pom pom for a nose. Dip the toothpick in black paint and dot two eyes. Use a toothpick as shown to comb out a mustache from the beard top.

actual height 3¾"

Santa Candy Basket

by Janet Kern Ward

one 3¼"x2"x1¾" chip basket with a 1½" tall
   handle
felt: 1"x1½" piece of pink, one 4"x2½" piece
   of red
two 10mm wiggle eyes
8" of ¼" wide green satin ribbon
pom poms: one ¼" wide red, one ¾" wide white
15" of ¾" wide naturally colored cotton fringe
tracing paper, pencil, ruler
low temperature glue gun and sticks or tacky
   craft glue

1 Trace the patterns. Cut one cheek piece from pink
felt and one hat from red felt. Glue the hat over the
basket handle. Glue the white pom pom to the handle
top. Glue the eyes ¼" apart ½" below the basket rim.
Glue the cheeks below the eyes.

2 Beard: Cut a 4½" length of fringe. Glue to the face
as shown, curving the ends to the rim of the basket.

3 Mustache: Unravel one fringe loop from the remaining fringe. Separate one strand and tie it around the
center of the remaining strands. Glue the mustache in
place, allowing the cheeks and a tiny mouth area to show.

4 Hair: Fold the remaining fringe in half to find the
center. Beginning at the fold, trim a ½" width of the
fringe to ½" long. Unfold—there will be a 1" area of
shorter "bangs" in the center. Glue the hair around the
basket rim, positioning the bangs over the eyes. Use the
ribbon to make a shoestring bow (see page 141) with ½"
loops and ¾" tails. Glue the bow to the left side of the
hair. Fill the basket with candy.

hat:
cut 1 red

cheeks: cut 1 pink

Cinnamon Stick Santa

by Judy Askins

one 10"–12" long cinnamon stick
one ½" wide wooden button ——————
acrylic paints: pale peach, black, red
¼" flat paintbrush
pink powdered blush, cotton swab
2" of red chenille stem
textured snow paint (such as Snow Accents™ or Snowtex™)
5" of naturally colored curly wool hair
low temperature glue gun and sticks or tacky craft glue

1 Measure 2½" from one end of the cinnamon stick and glue the wooden plug for the nose. Paint the plug and the stick ½"–¾" above and below the plug peach. Let dry, then dip the paintbrush handle in black paint and touch to the face to dot two eyes. Blush the cheeks.

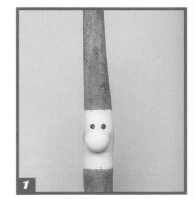

2 Paint the top red. Dab snow around the hat brim. Bend the chenille stem into a curve and glue into the top of the cinnamon stick for a hanger.

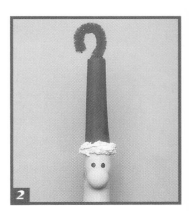

3 Pull out a 3" wisp of wool and glue crosswise under his nose, shaping it into a mustache. Bend the remaining wool in half and glue under the mustache for his beard.

actual height 13"

actual height 3¾"

Raggedy Santa
by Joan Zeigler

8"x4" of unbleached muslin fabric
5"x6" of lightweight plaid wool
4½" long craft stick
12" long stem of tan bumpy chenille
1" wide wood star
gold acrylic paint, ¼" flat paintbrush
18" of cream yarn
black fine-tip permanent pen (test on a fabric scrap)
pink powdered blush, cotton swab, round wooden toothpick
sewing machine, thread, hand sewing needle
polyester fiberfill
6" of nylon monofilament fishing line
low temperature glue gun and sticks or tacky craft glue

beard line

face line

fold line

hat

body

2 Fold the remaining muslin in half lengthwise and turn so the folded edge is at the top. Clip ¼" wide fringe; don't cut through the fold. Shake and fluff the fringe. Beginning at one side of the face, glue the fold along the beard line, straight across the back of the head, then once again along the beard line. Trim the back hair to 1" long. Knot one of the trimmed scraps in the center and glue for a mustache.

leave open

3 **Hat:** Sew the sides together in a ⅛" seam. Turn right side out and glue to the head, seam at the back. Glue chenille for a brim and around the body bottom. Glue the hat tip at one side. Knot two trimmed hair scraps together and cut the ends close to the knot. Glue the knot to the hat tip.

4 **Arms:** Cut a 1⅜" length from each end of the craft stick. Glue a ¼" hem in each sleeve, then glue around an arm so ¼" of the round end is exposed for the hand. Glue one arm to each side under the hair. Cut the yarn in half, hold the lengths together and tie around his waist. Paint the star gold and glue between the hands. Thread the fishline on the needle and take a stitch through the top fold of the hat. Knot the ends together to make a hanger.

Trace the patterns. Cut two bodies and two sleeves from wool. Place the hat pattern on the fold of the wool and cut one. Cut a 2"x4" muslin strip and fold crosswise into a square. Place the fold at the face line on the right side of one body piece, with the muslin extending up. Place the other body piece on top, right side down. Sew around the body in a ⅛" seam, leaving the bottom open. Trim the muslin to fit.

sleeve

1 Turn right side out and stuff with fiberfill. Tucking in the raw edges, sew a running stitch around the opening and gather tightly. Dip the toothpick in black paint and touch to the muslin to dot eyes. Blush the cheeks.

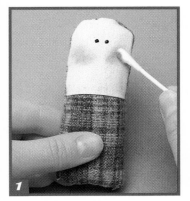

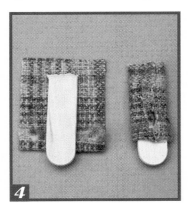

Woolly Santa

by Joan Zeigler

3" square of unbleached muslin fabric
5"x8" of lightweight plaid wool fabric
¾"x4½" piece of naturally colored curly lamb's wool
6" length of tan bumpy chenille stem
12" of jute twine
one ¼" wide gold jingle bell
black fine-tip permanent pen (test on a fabric scrap)
pink powdered blush, cotton swab
sewing machine, thread, hand sewing needle
polyester fiberfill
6" of nylon monofilament fishing line
low temperature glue gun and sticks or
     tacky craft glue

actual height 5"

1 Trace the patterns. Cut two bodies from wool and two faces from muslin. Place the body pieces right sides together and sew in a ⅛" seam, leaving open at the bottom. Clip the curves and turn right side out. Stuff firmly with fiberfill. Hand sew the opening closed.

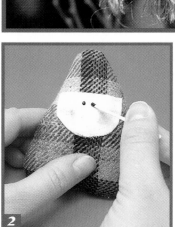

2 Glue the face pieces together (the double thickness prevents the wool from showing through). Dip the toothpick in black paint and touch to the muslin to dot each eye. Blush the cheeks. Glue to the body, placing the straight edge along the face line.

3 Tie the jute around his waist for a belt; knot each end. Glue the wool around his face as shown for a beard, trimming as necessary.

4 Glue the chenille around the head at the top of the face for a hat brim. Glue the bell to the tip of the hat. Thread the fishline on the needle and take a stitch through the top fold of the hat. Knot the ends together to make a hanger.

face line

body

face

leave open

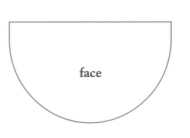

Santa in the Moon

by Nancy Overmyer

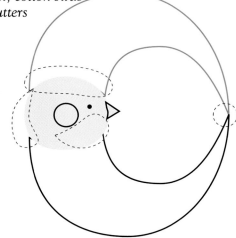

actual height 2½"

dough (see page 142): red, flesh, white
acrylic paints: black, white
round wooden toothpick
pink powdered blush, cotton swab
sharp knife, wire cutters
20-gauge wire
aluminum foil
baking sheet
polymer sealer
(such as Enviro-
tex® Lite)

1 Face: Form a ¾" ball of flesh dough and flatten slightly. **Beard:** Roll a 1" white dough ball into a 3" long teardrop. Cut ¼" off the round end. Use a toothpick to draw hair lines in the dough. Curve it into a C, moisten the cut end with water and attach to the head as shown.

2 Cheek: Flatten a ¼" flesh dough ball, moisten and press onto the face. **Nose:** Shape a ¼" flesh dough ball into a triangle. Moisten and press onto the face. **Mustache:** Form a ⅜" white dough ball into a teardrop, moisten and press onto the face, slightly overlapping the nose. Curve the tip; draw hair lines as for the beard.

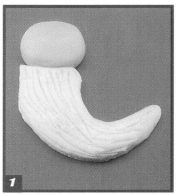

3 Hair: Form a ½" white dough ball into a teardrop. Flatten it slightly, moisten and press it onto the back of the head. Draw hair lines as before. **Hat:** Shape a 1" red dough ball as for the beard, but curve it the opposite way. Attach it to the top of the head, bringing the hat and beard tips together in a circle. Roll a ¼" white dough ball, moisten and attach at the join.

4 Hat brim: Roll a 1¼"x¼" white dough rope. Moisten it and press around the base of the hat. Form the wire into a loop, twist the ends together and insert into the top curve of the hat for a hanger. Bake at 325° for 2–3 hours until completely hard. Dip the toothpick into black paint to dot the eye. Blush the cheek. Use the toothpick dipped in white paint to draw stars on the hat. Let dry. Seal (see page 142).

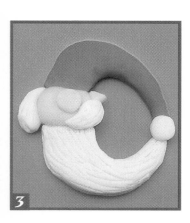

Dough Santa Pin

by Nancy Overmyer

actual height of Santa 2"

dough (see page 42): red, flesh, white
¾ yard of 1 ⅜" wide red/green plaid taffeta
  ribbon
acrylic paints: black, white
1 ½" long pin back
round wooden toothpick
pink powdered blush, cotton swab
sharp knife, wire cutters, 6" of 30-gauge wire
aluminum foil, baking sheet
polymer sealer (such as Envirotex® Lite)
low temperature glue gun and sticks or tacky
  craft glue

1 **Head:** Slightly flatten a ¾" ball of flesh dough. **Beard:** Roll a ½" white ball into a 2½" long rope with pointed ends. Moisten with water and wrap around the lower head. Use the toothpick to make hair lines.

2 **Mustache:** Shape two ⅜" white balls into ½" teardrops. Moisten and attach point to point as shown. Use the toothpick to indent a line in the center of each. **Nose:** Mix a pinch of red dough with an equal part of flesh. Roll a ⅛" ball of this mix and attach over the mustache points.

3 **Hat:** Roll a 1" red ball into a 2½" long teardrop. Indent the round end, moisten and press it onto the head. Roll a ¼"x1½" white log and wrap around the hat base. Roll a ¼" white ball and press to the hat tip. Pull the tip down and press it to the brim as shown. Bake at 325° for 2–3 hours until completely hard. Dip the toothpick in black paint to dot each eye. Blush the cheeks. Seal (see page 142).

4 **Pin:** Use the plaid ribbon to make an oblong bow (see page 140) with two 2" loops, two 2½" loops and 3" tails. Do not cut the wire. Open the pin and glue to the back of the bow; wrap the wire 2–3 times around the pin for extra security, then trim the wire. Glue the Santa to the bow front.

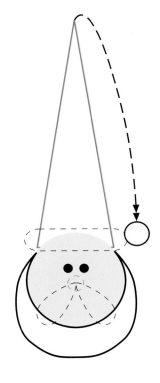

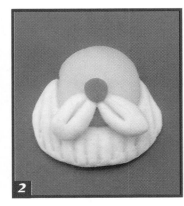

Soft-Serve Santa

by Nancy Overmyer and LeNae Gerig

polymer clay (see page 143): pale
*   peach, white, burgundy*
acrylic paints: black, white
#0 liner paintbrush
pink powdered blush, cotton swab
9" of gold cord
1 ½" length of 20-gauge wire
sharp knife, pliers
round wooden toothpick
glass or ceramic baking dish

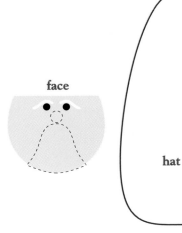

face

hat

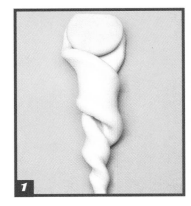

1

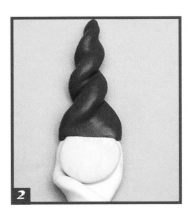

2

actual height 6½"

beard

3

1 **Beard:** Roll a 1¼" white clay ball into a 4" long teardrop. Flatten slightly and twist into a spiral as shown, leaving the rounded top untwisted. Indent the top with your fingertip. **Face:** Flatten a ½" peach ball to 1" wide and press into the indentation. Cut ¼" off the top of the beard and head.

2 **Hat:** Roll a 1" burgundy ball into a 2½" long teardrop and shape as for the beard, but without the flattened end. Cut ¼" off the rounded end. Press onto the head.

3 **Brim:** Roll a ¼"x1½" white log and wrap it around the hat base. **Mustache:** Flatten a ¼" white ball to match the pattern. Press onto the bottom of the face. Use the knife to draw hair lines.

4 Form the wire into a loop and twist the ends together. Insert the twisted ends into an upper twist of the hat for a hanger. Follow the clay manufacturer's instructions to bake, or bake at 250° for 45 minutes to an hour. Dip the toothpick in black paint to dot each eye. Use the liner brush to paint the eyebrows white. Blush the cheeks and nose. Loop the cord through the wire hanger and knot the ends.

4

Old-Fashioned Santa

by Lori Anderson

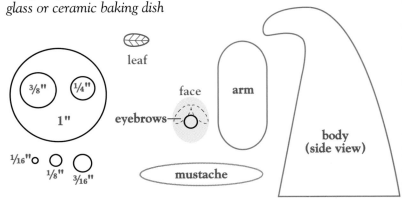

beard

leaf

face

eyebrows

arm

mustache

body (side view)

3/8" 1/4"

1"

1/16"o 1/8" 3/16"

polymer clay (see page 143): red, white, green, light peach, black
2" of 18-gauge wire
sharp knife
glass or ceramic baking dish

actual height 2⅝"

1 **Body:** Shape a 1½" ball of red clay into a cone, bending the tip back as shown in the pattern. **Arms:** Cut a 1" red ball in half and shape each half into a 1" long log. Slightly flatten one end of each and press to the shoulders. Curve the arms forward. **Mittens:** Roll a ¼" green ball, cut in half and attach one half to the end of each arm. Pinch to flatten slightly.

2 **Face:** Flatten a ¼" peach ball into an oval and press onto the top front of the cone where it begins to curve backward. Attach a ⅛" flesh ball for the nose. **Robe trim:** Roll a ¼"x6" white rope. Cut a 1" length, flatten slightly and attach at the robe front. Wrap the rest of the rope around the robe bottom, joining and smoothing the ends in the back. Roll two ⅛"x1½" white ropes and attach one around each cuff.

3 **Hood trim:** Roll a ⅛"x3" white rope and attach it in a circle around the face. **Eyebrows:** Roll two ⅛"x½" white ropes. Flatten each and attach diagonally above his nose. Use the knife to imprint hair lines. **Beard:** Roll a ⅜"x1½" white rope and flatten to 2" long. Imprint hair lines, then attach below his nose, curling the lower end to one side. **Mustache:** Roll a ¼"x¾" white rope, flatten and point the ends. Imprint hair lines. Twist into a spiral and attach at the beard top.

4 **Holly:** Roll eight 3/16" green balls and flatten to match the leaf pattern. Use the knife to imprint vein lines, then attach to the hood trim as shown. Roll three 1/16" red balls and attach for berries. **Walking stick:** Insert the wire through the left mitten until it touches the table. Cover with small pieces of black clay, keeping the surface lumpy and rough like an old stick. Follow the clay manufacturer's instructions to bake, or bake at 250° for 45 minutes to an hour. Allow to cool completely before handling.

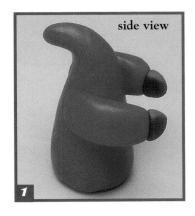

side view

1

2

3

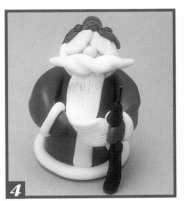

4

Tie Dolly Santa

by Delores Ruzicka

1 red or burgundy men's tie, at least 2½" wide
one 6" tall Styrofoam® cone
one 1¾" round wooden ball
two ½" round wooden beads
handful of naturally colored curly wool
acrylic paints: light peach, black, white
paintbrushes: #6 flat, #00 liner
one 9" long twig
1"x30" strip of brown acrylic fur
30-gauge wire
pink powdered blush, cotton swab
strong white thread
low temperature glue gun and sticks or tacky craft glue

1 Paint the 1¾" ball peach and the ½" beads black; let dry and recoat if needed. Transfer (see page 143) the face pattern to the 1¾" ball and paint as shown. Blush his cheeks.

2 Cut the tie as shown in the diagram at left. Open the robe piece and wrap it around the cone. Glue it around the top and down the opening edges (if the tie is too narrow to meet in front, the fur will cover the gap).

3 Glue the sleeves to the back ½" below the neck. Glue a black bead into the end of each sleeve. Glue the head to the top of the cone.

4 Cut a 9½" fur length and glue it around the robe bottom. Cut a 5½" fur length and glue it down the center front. Glue the hands to the robe front fur. Cut two 1½" fur lengths and glue one to the front of each cuff. **Mustache:** Cut a ½"x2" wool piece. Wrap the center with thread and knot. Glue under the nose. Glue the remaining wool as shown for his hair and beard. Glue the twig under his right arm as shown in the large photo.

actual height 8"

discard | sleeves | discard | robe | discard
← 7" →   ← 7" →

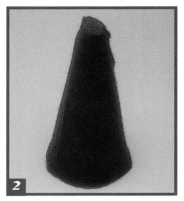

Mr. & Mrs. Santa Bunny by Nancy Overmyer

1 size small left-handed natural cotton glove
(see page 59 to use the other glove)
one 4½"x6"x2½" red wicker basket
1 yard of 1½" wide red/green plaid ribbon
9" of ⅛" wide red satin ribbon
3" of 1" wide white lace
4" square of Christmas print fabric
1 green silk fir branch with twelve 5" long sprigs
3¾" of 22-gauge gold wire
1½"x2½" piece of red felt
4" of ¼" wide white ivory rope braid
one ½" wide white pom pom
ten 3½" and two 2" lengths of natural cotton string
small-eyed and large-eyed hand sewing needles
black fine-tip permanent pen (test on a fabric scrap)
acrylic paints: green, red
low temperature glue gun and sticks or tacky craft glue
polyester fiberfill
sewing machine
white thread

face (both bunnies)

actual height 8"

1 Cut off the glove cuff. Sew the front and back together in a straight line from between the middle fingers to the center bottom. Gather the two left fingers together at the base and wrap tightly with thread; knot to secure. Repeat with the two right fingers—these will be the bunnies' ears. Cut off and discard the thumb; tuck the raw edges inside. Softly stuff each half of the hand area, then sew the bottom closed.

2 Mr. Bunny: Refer to the pattern to paint the face on the left bunny, placing the top 1" below the base of the ears. Draw the mouth with a black pen. Thread a 2" string length onto a large-eyed needle and take a stitch between the nose and mouth. Set the needle aside and adjust the string so the ends are equal. Fray the ends to form whiskers. Hold all the 3½" string lengths together, wrap the centers tightly with thread and knot to secure. Glue the knot under his mouth for a beard. Trace the hat pattern and cut one of red felt. Fold in half along the straight edge and glue together, forming a cone. Glue onto his head. Glue the rope braid around the brim and the pom pom to the tip. Glue a 2" fir tip into the thumb hole.

hat

3 Mrs. Bunny: Paint her face and make her whiskers as for Mr. Bunny. Bend the wire around a pencil as shown to make her glasses. Push the wire ends into the glove so the glasses rest over her eyes. Sew a running stitch along the bound edge of the lace and gather it tightly. Glue at the base of her ears. Use the ⅛" ribbon to make a shoestring bow (see page 141) with ½" loops and ¾" tails. Glue to the top of the lace. Fold the fabric square diagonally and glue for her shawl.

glasses

4 Bend the fir branch to fit inside the basket, curving the sprigs along the rim. Use the plaid ribbon to make a puffy bow with a center loop, four 3½" loops and 4" tails. Glue to the left rim of the basket as shown in the large photo. Glue the bunnies into the basket center.

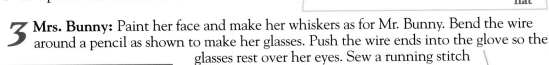

Clothespin Santa

by Loyal Hjelmervik

fabric: 11" square of Christmas print, 3"x4" of unbleached muslin,
*   4"x8" of black broadcloth, 3"x4" of white fur*
white Mini Curl™ curly hair
acrylic paints: black, white
#1 round paintbrush
one 3" long wooden spring clothespin
one 2½" tall Christmas tree
one 10mm gold jingle bell
pink powdered blush, cotton swab
polyester fiberfill
sewing machine or needle and thread
tracing paper, transfer paper, pencil
low temperature glue gun and sticks or tacky craft glue

actual height 7"

fold line:

body

leg

arm

suit

sleeve

hat

1 (All seams are ¼".) **Body:** Transfer the body pattern to doubled muslin fabric; cut out. Place the pieces right sides together and sew, leaving the bottom open. Clip curves, turn right side out and stuff firmly. Sew the opening closed. Paint the eyes black with white highlights. Blush the cheeks. **Arms, legs:** Trace the patterns, place on doubled black fabric and cut out; turn over and repeat for a total of four leg and four arm pieces. Place two legs together and sew, leaving the end open. Clip curves, turn right side out and stuff firmly. Sew the opening closed. Repeat for the remaining leg and the arms.

2 **Suit:** Trace the suit, sleeve and hat patterns. Place the print fabric right side up and fold the edges in to the center. Lay the patterns on the fabric with the fold lines of the suit and sleeves on fabric folds. Cut out. Repeat for another suit and sleeve. Sew each sleeve along the edge opposite the fold, forming a tube. Sew the hat along both long edges, leaving the bottom open. Open the suit pieces flat, place right sides together and sew along both sides from the crotch point to the top. Refold with the inseams together and sew from ankle to ankle. Clip the crotch curve and trim the top hat point. Turn all the pieces right side out.

3 Pin a sleeve to one side of the suit, centering the seam. Sew; repeat on the other side. Sew a running stitch around the neck edge; repeat at each wrist and ankle. Glue the body into the suit, pull the stitching tight around the neck and knot to secure. Glue an arm into each wrist and a leg into each ankle. Pull up and knot the stitching.

4 Glue on the hat. Cut the fur into ¼" wide strips and glue around the wrists, ankles and hat brim. Glue on the hair and beard as shown in the large photo. Glue the tree between his hands. Glue the bell to the hat tip, bring it down and glue it to one side. Glue the clothespin to his bottom as if he were sitting on it.

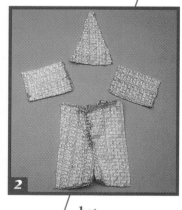

Around the World

by Dawn Quick

3"x2" round wicker basket with a 2" tall handle
3¼"x2¼" of unbleached muslin fabric
1"x10" of green/cream checked fabric
2"x3" of burgundy broadcloth fabric
2⅜" tall wooden doll peg———————
acrylic paints: pale peach, burgundy, black
#2 flat paintbrush
three 3" long sprigs of green silk fir
⅜" wide silver jingle bell
1" length of naturally colored curly wool
polyester fiberfill
12" of jute twine
tan thread
tracing paper, pencil
low temperature glue gun and sticks or tacky craft glue

1 Paint the doll head peach and the body burgundy; let dry. Dip the handle of the paintbrush in black paint and dot each eye. **Hat:** Trace the pattern and cut one from the burgundy fabric. Turn under the bottom edge ⅛" and glue, then fold the hat right sides together and glue the long edges together in a ¼" seam. Turn right side out and glue onto the head. Fold the top to the left and glue inside the fold to hold it in place.

2 Beard: Fluff the hair. Separate a strand and set aside. Glue the rest as shown for his beard, then glue the last strand crosswise for his mustache. Glue Santa into the left side of the basket.

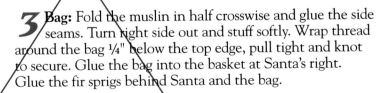

3 Bag: Fold the muslin in half crosswise and glue the side seams. Turn right side out and stuff softly. Wrap thread around the bag ¼" below the top edge, pull tight and knot to secure. Glue the bag into the basket at Santa's right. Glue the fir sprigs behind Santa and the bag.

4 Insert a doubled thread through the loop of the bell and tie it to the bottom right basket handle. Knot the checked fabric strip around the handle just above the bell, then tie in a shoestring bow (see page 141) with 1" loops and 1" tails. For a hanger, knot the ends of the jute together, then loop it around the basket handle in a lark's head knot.

hat

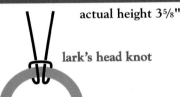

actual height 3⅝"

lark's head knot

A Collection of Santas 🎅 **39**

actual height 5⅜"

Kris Klaus
by Dawn Quick

¼ yard of unbleached muslin fabric
6" square of red/green plaid fabric
1 ½" long sprig of green silk fir
20" of jute twine
one ⅜" wide silver jingle bell
acrylic paints: black, white
#0 liner paintbrush, round wooden toothpick
pink powdered blush, cotton swab
needle, cream thread
polyester fiberfill
tracing paper, transfer paper, pencil
low temperature glue gun and sticks or tacky
    craft glue

beard line

1 Fold the muslin in half. Transfer (see page 143) the head pattern onto the muslin and cut out through both layers. Paint the features black. Dip a toothpick in white paint to dot highlights in each eye. Let dry. Place the painted circle right side down on the other one and sew together in a ¼" seam, leaving 1" open at the top. Clip the curves, turn, and stuff. Sew the opening closed. Blush the cheeks.

2 **Beard:** Cut a 6"x16" muslin strip and fold in half lengthwise. Cut into ¼"–⅜" wide fringe; don't cut through the fold. Sew a running stitch near the fold and pull to gather around his head, following the beard line and overlapping the ends in back. Glue in place.
Mustache: Cut three ¼"x2" muslin strips and hold together. Wrap thread tightly around the centers, knot and glue over the center top of the beard.

3 **Hat:** Trace the pattern and cut from plaid fabric. Fold along the fold line, right sides together, and sew a ¼" seam along the straight edges. Glue the hat onto his head with the seam at the back. For a hanger, cut a 12" jute length. Fold it in half and glue the cut ends to the bottom of the hat seam.

4 **Brim:** Cut a ¾"x20" muslin strip. Sew a running stitch lengthwise down the center. Pull the threads, gathering the strip to fit around the lower edge of the hat. Glue in place, overlapping the ends at the back. Pull the hat tip down and glue to the left side of the brim. Glue the bell to the hat tip. Glue the fir sprig to the other side of the brim. Use the remaining jute to tie a shoestring bow (see page 141) with ¾" loops and ¾" tails. Glue over the bottom of the fir.

fold line

back view

Santa on Wood

by Nancy Overmyer

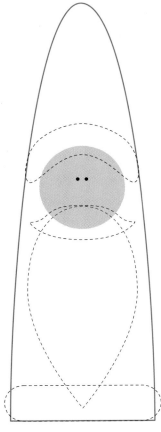

actual height 5"

dough (see page 142): white, red, pink
5"x½" round crosscut wood piece with bark
one 4½" long sprig of green artificial pine with 2" long needles
1 yard of ⅞" wide red plaid ribbon
24-gauge wire

handful of Spanish moss
black acrylic paint, polymer sealer
sharp knife, round wooden toothpick
low temperature glue gun and sticks or tacky craft glue

1 Roll a 2" ball of red dough into a 4½" tall cone. With your finger, indent 2" below the top. Flatten a ½" pink ball to ⅞" wide, moisten with water and attach in the indentation.

2 Roll a ⅜"x7½" white rope. Cut a 3" length, moisten above the face and wrap as shown, joining the ends in back. Attach the rest around the base, joining with water.

3 **Beard:** Roll a 1" white ball into a 2½" long teardrop. Flatten slightly and use the knife to imprint hair lines. Attach with water to the bottom of the face and the front of the body. **Mustache:** Flatten a ⅝" white ball to match the pattern and imprint as for the beard. Curl the tips upward.

4 With water, attach the mustache over the beard top. Bake at 325° until hard; let cool. Dip the toothpick into black paint and touch to the face to dot eyes. Let dry; seal (see page 142). Glue Santa to the wood, slightly left of center, with the pine next to him for a tree. Use the ribbon to make a loopy bow (see page 140) with six 2" loops and 4" tails. Glue as shown. Glue moss around Santa and the tree as shown in the large photo above.

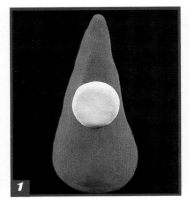

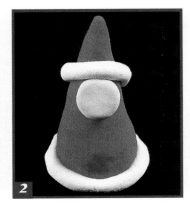

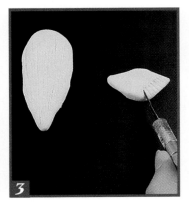

side view

An Armful of Angels

Angels have always been a favorite decoration for Christmas, adorning the tree top and limbs, sitting among greenery on the mantel or as focal points of gorgeous evergreen wreaths. And they come in all sizes, dressed in simple, ragged-edged clothing or in the finest brocades and trims.

Lately, we've seen angels used in decorating to stay up year-round. It all started with celestial decorating using stars, moons and suns, gloriously displayed on dark blue or black backgrounds. We naturally progressed to angels (also "celestial bodies"), encouraged by all the "guardian angels" who suddenly appeared everywhere. Today we see all sorts of angels, including garden angels, angels to guard the home and kitchen angels.

The angels featured in this section have all been made with Christmas decorating in mind. However, we're sure they wouldn't mind if you wanted to change them into everyday angels. Their clothing could be changed to everyday colors. Or, instead of making them as ornaments, use one as a decoration on a wreath created for your kitchen or entryway. Some of these beauties are best shown at Christmastime, but others would adapt very well to changes.

However you choose to use these ladies, all will enhance any decor, whether at Christmastime or throughout the year.

Paper Ribbon Treetop Angel

by Susan Luke

one 1 5⁄8" round wooden bead
one 2 1⁄4" wide wooden star
1 2⁄3 yards of 4" wide white twisted paper ribbon
1 yard of 2 1⁄2" wide cream gathered lace
6" of 1⁄4" wide white satin ribbon
24" of 6mm ivory fused pearls
eleven 3⁄8" wide white ribbon roses
black fine-tip permanent pen
handful of strawberry blonde Mini Curl™ curly hair
acrylic paints: dark blue, pink, white, metallic gold
paintbrushes: #00 liner, #10 flat
paper towels
tracing paper, transfer paper, pencil
10" square of heavy paper
needle, strong thread
low temperature glue gun and sticks or tacky craft glue

actual height 11 1⁄2"

1. Transfer (see page 143) the face pattern to one side of the bead. Use the pen to outline the eyes, eyelashes, nose and mouth. Paint the irises blue. Load the flat brush with pink, dab off most of the paint on a paper towel and paint the cheeks. Paint the whites of her eyes, the star highlights and the cheek highlights white. Use the pen to dot her freckles.

2. Untwist all the paper ribbon. Cut five 10" lengths and glue side by side along the 10" edges to form a 20"x10" rectangle. Use the same technique as for the cheeks to dry-brush with gold paint; let dry. Fold in half crosswise, then in thirds to form a 3 1⁄3"x10" rectangle. Cut one 3 1⁄3" end into a curve, then unfold—there will be six equal scallops.

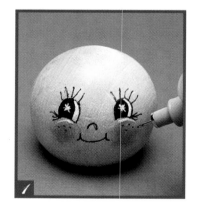

3. Glue the bound edge of the lace to the back of the paper ribbon just above the notch of the scallops. Bring the 10" sides together, overlapping the edges 1⁄4" to form a tube; glue.

4. **Base:** Trace the pattern from page 45, placing the fold line on the fold of the tracing paper. Unfold and cut from heavy paper. Overlap the straight edges 1⁄4" and glue, forming a cone. Glue lace around the bottom of the cone as shown; trim excess.

5 Put the paper ribbon tube over the cone. Gather the top slightly and glue in place. Glue on the head.

6 Sew a running stitch through the bound edge of the remaining lace, gather it tightly around her neck and glue in place for a collar.

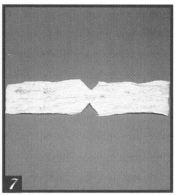

7 **Arms:** Cut a 14" length of paper ribbon and notch as shown. Dry-brush with gold as for the dress.

8 Paint the star gold. Twist the center of the arms and glue to the back of the star. Glue the ends of the arms to her back under the collar, overlapping them ¼".

9 **Wings:** Cut 36" of paper ribbon and use to make a loopy bow (see page 140) with two 4½" loops and 7" tails. Trim each tail in an inverted V. Glue to the back of the collar as shown.

10 **Hair:** Cut the hair into 3"–6" lengths. Glue to the top, back and sides of the head. **Halo:** Glue a 4" length of pearls in a circle on top of her head. Glue four ribbon roses along the front of the halo. Use the ribbon to make a shoestring bow with ¾" loops and 1½" tails. Glue at her chin with a rose in the center.

back view

11 Beginning at the center back, glue the remaining pearls along the scalloped edge of the skirt. Glue a rose at the top of each scallop as shown.

fold line

**cone for base:
cut 1 of heavy paper**

Rita Rabbit

by Dawn Quick

¼ yard of unbleached muslin fabric
1 ¼" square of burgundy calico fabric
12" of 2" wide mauve cinnamay ribbon
12" of ¹⁄₁₆" wide mauve satin ribbon
two 4mm black beads
one ¾"x1" natural wicker basket with handle
one ½" long artificial fir sprig
12" of jute twine
embroidery floss: pink, cream
darning needle, cream and black thread
polyester fiberfill
tracing paper, pencil
low temperature glue gun and sticks or tacky craft glue

3½" circle

actual height 6"

1 Trace the patterns. **Head:** Cut a 3½" muslin circle. Sew a running stitch ¼" from the edge and pull to gather. Stuff until the head measures 1¼" across, then pull the threads to close the opening. Knot to secure. Pinch the head to shape a pointed nose in the front. Embroider a pink Y on the nose. Sew on the beads for eyes. **Whiskers:** Thread the needle with two strands of cream embroidery floss. Take a stitch from top to bottom through one whisker point, leaving a ½" tail. Stitch again and cut the floss ½" away. Repeat on the other side.

back view

2 **Ears:** Cut one piece from muslin; knot the center. Glue the knot to the top of the head. **Body:** Tear an 8" muslin square. Fold in half diagonally and knot 1" from each folded corner to form hands. Cut a heart from calico and sew to the dress as shown with ¼" long black stitches.

3 Cut a 1½" opening (see diagram) in the center of the folded edge. Sew a running stitch around the edges of the opening and pull to gather. Glue the gathers to the bottom of the head. **Wings:** Fold the ends of the mesh ribbon in to overlap 1" at the center. Tie the center with the jute, making a shoestring bow (see page 141) with 1" loops and 4" tails. Glue the wings to the body back.

4 Glue the fir sprig into the basket. Glue the hands through the handle. Use the ¹⁄₁₆" ribbon to make a shoestring bow with ¾" loops and 3½" tails. Glue it at the neck as shown in the large photo. Thread the needle with cream embroidery floss and take a stitch through the back of her head. Trim the tails to 5" and knot the ends together for a hanger..

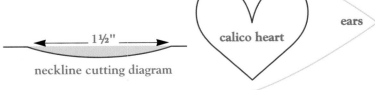

1½"

neckline cutting diagram

calico heart

ears

Candle Cup Cutie

by Marilyn Gossett

one 1¼" tall wooden candle cup
one 1" wide wooden button
⅔ yard of ⅜" wide pink satin ribbon
½ yard of 1½" wide white moiré ribbon
⅛ yard of 1½" wide white gathered lace
four ½" wide pink ribbon roses
small handful of blonde Mini Curl™ curly hair
7" of ⅛" wide gold cord
6" of gold thread
acrylic paints: pale peach, pink
¼" flat paintbrush
fine-tip black permanent pen
gold glitter dimensional paint
pink powdered blush, cotton swab
24-gauge wire
tracing paper, transfer paper, pencil
low temperature glue gun and sticks
   or tacky craft glue

actual height 7"

1 Paint the candle cup pink and the button peach; let dry. Squeeze four dots of glitter onto the candle cup front for buttons. Transfer (see page 143) the face pattern to the button and go over the lines with the pen. Blush the cheeks. Cut 15" of pink ribbon and fold in half. Turn the candle cup upside down. Push the fold into the cup and through the hole, pulling ⅞" out at the top. Glue the button to the fold, facing forward. Knot 1" from each ribbon end and glue a rose below each knot. Trim the ends round for the toes of her shoes.

2 **Arms:** Knot the center of the remaining pink ribbon. Glue the ends to the top back of the candle cup so the knot forms clasped hands. Glue a rose to the hands. **Skirt:** Glue the bound edge of the lace around the lower edge of the candle cup. Glue the gold cord over the binding and trim excess cord.

3 **Wings:** Use the white ribbon to make a loopy bow (see page 140) with two 2" loops and 2" tails. Trim each tail in an inverted V. Glue it to her back; glue the last rose to the center of the bow.

4 Insert the gold thread through the ribbon loop at the back of her head. Knot the ends to form a hanger. Cut 2½" hair lengths and glue to her head—fluff and trim as necessary. Form the remaining gold cord into a 1" circle and glue for a halo.

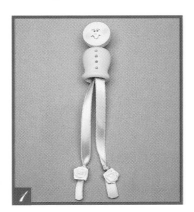

back view

Flower Angel
by Loyal Hjelmervik

1 white silk rose stem with a 3" wide rose and
    two 1¾" long green leaves
one 1" round wood bead with a ¼" hole
one ¼" wide white ribbon rose
12" of ¼" wide red satin ribbon
8" of gold wired mini star garland
10" of nylon monofilament fishing line
needle with a large eye
small handful of Spanish moss
gold glitter spray
fabric stiffener
low temperature glue gun and sticks or tacky
    craft glue

actual height 2¾"

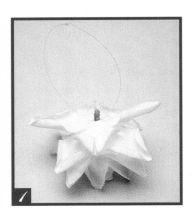

1 **Body:** Dip the rose into fabric stiffener. Pull two bottom petals up and twist forward for her arms. Hang upside down overnight or until dry. Remove any remaining drops of stiffener. Remove the calyx and leaves; cut the stem to ¼". For a hanger, thread the needle with the fishing line and take a stitch through the flower base. Knot the ends of the line together.

2 **Head:** Insert the fishing line and stem through the bead hole. Glue the bead to the flower, then glue moss as shown for hair.

3 **Wings:** Cut the stems of two leaves to ½" long. Glue the leaves to the back of her neck extending outward as shown. Cut the ribbon into two 6" lengths and use each to tie a shoestring bow (see page 141) with ¾" loops and 1" tails. Glue one to the center of her wings and the other under her chin.

4 Glue the ribbon rose to the center of the neck bow.
Halo: Wrap the garland around your fingers, forming a 1½" circle. Glue it to her hair. Lightly mist the entire angel with glitter spray.

back view

Two Little Angels Treasure Box

by LeNae Gerig

4½"x6½" papier-mâché recipe box
¼ yard of 45" wide ivory satin fabric
ivory spray paint
ivory crocheted scalloped round doilies:
    one 6", one 8"
1⅓ yards of ½" wide ivory self-adhesive gimp braid
one 3½" long ivory tassel
one 4½"x6" ivory postcard with 2 angels
⅛" wide satin ribbon: 1¼ yard each white, ivory
⅔ yard of ⅛" wide ivory rope braid
one ⅜" wide gold button
26-gauge wire, spray adhesive
low temperature glue gun and sticks, tacky craft glue

1 Spray the inside and outside of the box and lid ivory; let dry. Cut the fabric into three pieces: 4¾"x6¾", 3¾"x23" and 7"x8½".

2 Spray the box bottom with adhesive. Center the wrong side of the 4¾"x6¾" piece on it and press in place. Spray the box sides with adhesive and smooth the fabric edges up, folding out excess at the corners. Wrap the 23" strip around the box sides with the seams meeting at a back corner. Spray the lid and cover with the 7"x8½" piece, mitering the corners as shown.

3 Cut each doily in half between scallops. Use tacky glue to attach one large half around the front right corner, positioning the cut edge even with the box bottom. Repeat with the other large half around the lower back left corner. Glue the small halves around the front left and back right corners, placing the cut edges even with the top. Starting at a back corner, adhere half the gimp around the box bottom. Adhere the other half around the lower edge of the lid with the bottom scallops extending past the rim; cut off excess.

4 Use the glue gun to attach the card centered on the box top. Glue rope braid around the card edge. Glue the loop of the tassel to the front center of the lid. Hold the ribbons together and make a loopy bow (see page 140) with six 2" loops of each color and 4½" tails. Glue over the tassel loop. Knot the ends of the bow tails and glue the button to the bow center.

Angel Candle

by Teri Stillwaugh

3"x9" white pillar candle
4½" tall white battenburg angel
4" round white battenburg doily
1 Tbsp. of Liquitex Model Magic® clay
2½" yards of metallic silver garland with clear iridescent stars
handful of white iridescent glitter
acrylic paints: black, white, mauve
dimensional paints: metallic gold, white glitter
matte acrylic sealer
#8 flat paintbrush, round wooden toothpick
low temperature glue gun and sticks or tacky craft glue

1 Seal the candle; let dry. Glue the angel centered on one side. Apply glue to the sleeves and dress, then sprinkle with glitter. Let dry.

2 Mix Model Magic® with two drops of mauve paint. **Head:** Form a ⅞"x¼" circle. **Hands:** Form two ⅜" balls. Glue the head to the dress top and the hands between the sleeves, overlapping them as shown.

3 Use a toothpick to paint a mauve circle for the mouth, black circles for eyes, and black eyelashes. Make a white dot in the mouth and one in each eye. For the hair, squiggle gold paint as shown.

4 Cut 36 stars from the garland and glue evenly spaced all over the candle. Squeeze a white glitter dot on the center of each star. Glue the candle in the doily center. Coil the garland loosely around the base. Twist the end loosely around the coils at the back, then glue the twisted area to the candle and doily. Add white glitter dots evenly spaced to the wings and dress trim as shown; let dry. Seal.

back view of candle base

Block Baby Angel

by Marilyn Gossett

⅛ yard of brown broadcloth fabric
1 yard of white broadcloth fabric
3"x3¼"x1½" wooden block
one 9½" round white battenburg doily
handful of black Maxi-Curl™ curly hair
1 yard of 1" wide white gathered lace
1½ yards of 1" wide white flat lace
1 yard of 3½" wide white flat lace
1 white chenille stem
#00 liner paintbrush
round wooden toothpick
fabric marker with disappearing ink
tracing paper, transfer paper, pencil
black fine-tip permanent pen
2 yards of ¼" wide white satin ribbon
1¼ yards of ⅜" wide white satin picot
   ribbon
acrylic paints: pink, dark pink,
   brown, black, white
sewing machine, needle
brown and white thread
polyester fiberfill
low temperature glue gun
   and sticks or tacky craft glue

actual height 12"

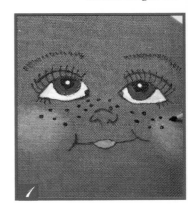

1 Trace the patterns from this page and
page 53. From brown fabric cut two face
pieces, two head pieces, four hands and four
feet. Transfer (see page 143) the face pattern
to one face piece. With the black pen, go over
all the lines and fill in the eye pupil and inner
corner. Paint the irises brown and the mouth
dark pink. Lightly brush pink onto the
cheeks. Dip the toothpick into white
paint, then touch to each eye to dot
white highlights. Dot black freckles
in the same way. Let dry.

head:
cut 2 of brown

leave this end open

face:
cut 2 of brown
paint 1

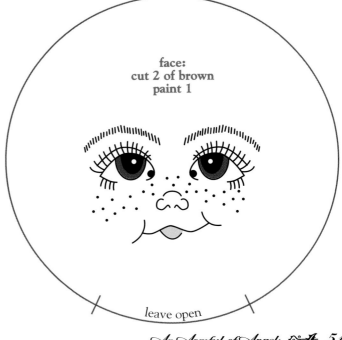

leave open

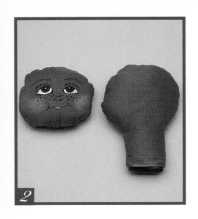

2 Pin the painted face to the other face piece, right sides together. Sew with a ¼" seam, leaving the bottom open. Clip curves, turn right side out and stuff firmly. Hand sew the opening closed. Sew, turn and stuff the head/neck pieces in the same way, leaving open at the bottom and for ½" up each side.

3 Glue the face to the head front. Squeeze out a 1" circle of glue (hot glue works best) onto the top of the wood block and press the neck opening into the glue. Pull the fabric edges down over the block and glue securely.

4 **For each sleeve:** Cut a 7"x8½" piece of white fabric. Press under ½" on one 7" edge. Cut a 7" length of 1" flat lace and lay it along the edge with the top at the raw edge of the fabric. Stitch ⅜" from the fold through all three layers, forming a casing. Fold the sleeve in half lengthwise, right sides together, and sew a ¼" seam, leaving open at the casing. Turn right side out.

Romper (see diagram A): Cut two from white fabric, placing the fold line of the pattern on the fold of the fabric. Mark the fold line with a snip or pin, then open up each piece. Sew them together along one crotch seam. Clip the curve and lay the pieces flat, right side up, with the seam in the center. Fold each sleeve so the seam is at the center back and pin one to the center of each side, matching the seam to the fold line.

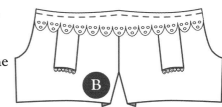

(Diagram B) Sew the 3½" lace to the upper edge of the romper with a ⅝" seam, right sides up and raw edges even, catching the sleeves in the stitching.

5 Fold the raw edges to the inside along the stitching line, lifting the sleeves and lace up out of the way. Sew ½" away from the first stitching, forming a casing.

6 Lay the romper wrong side up and press a ½" hem in the lower edge of each leg. Lay 1" lace on one leg with the top at the raw edge and stitch ⅜" away, forming a casing. Trim excess lace and repeat for the other leg. Fold the romper right sides together and sew the other crotch seam, leaving an opening at the upper casing. Refold the romper so the inseams are together, matching the crotch seams. Sew the inseam from ankle to ankle, leaving an opening at each casing. Turn right side out; press.

7 Cut 24" of ¼" ribbon. Insert it through the neck casing. Slip the body inside the romper and pull the ribbon ends to gather the neck tightly. Knot in back, then tie in a shoestring bow (see page 141) with 1¼" loops and 2" tails.

8 **Pinafore:** Cut a 7"x36" piece of white fabric. Sew a ¼" hem on each 7" edge. Press under ¼" on one long edge, then sew the bound edge of the gathered lace over it. Sew a running stitch along the remaining long edge and pull the threads to gather the pinafore tightly around the doll, under the sleeves. Knot at the back to secure.

top
back
view

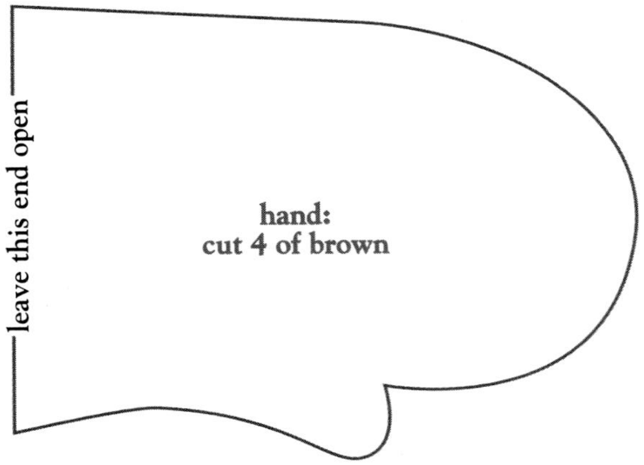

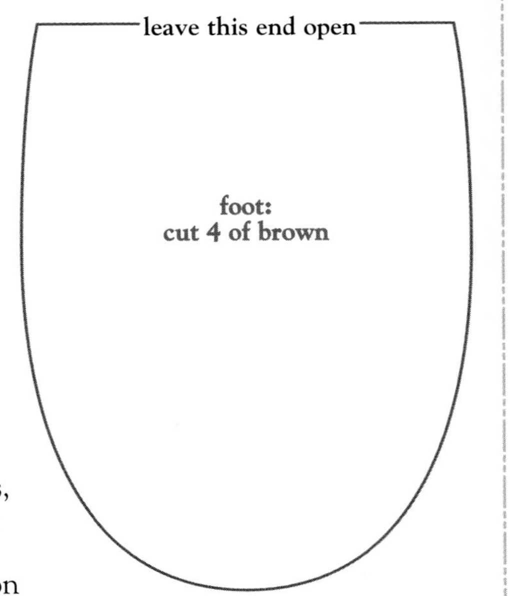

hand:
cut 4 of brown

leave this end open

foot:
cut 4 of brown

leave this end open

crotch seam

9 **For each hand:** Sew two pieces together in a ⅛" seam, leaving the straight end open. Clip the curves, turn right side out and stuff. Lightly stuff the sleeve. Cut 12" of ¼" ribbon and insert through one wrist casing. Glue the hand into the sleeves, thumb up. Pull the ribbon to gather the cuff around the wrist. Knot, then tie in a shoestring bow with ¾" loops and 1" tails.

10 Lightly stuff the romper. **Feet:** Make, glue and tie into the ankle cuffs as for the hands.

11 **Wings:** Pinch the center of the doily and wire to secure. Glue to the back of her collar. Use 12" of ¼" ribbon to make a shoestring bow with 1" loops and 3" tails. Glue to the wired area of the wings.

12 **Hair:** Stretch a handful of hair to 9" long. Glue the center to the top front of the head. Working toward the back, repeat for the desired coverage. Tack the hair in place in the back and sides with small dabs of glue. Fluff and trim. **Halo:** Form the chenille stem into a 3" circle and bend the rest down at a right angle. Wrap the stem spiral-fashion with picot ribbon, completely covering it. Glue the straight end to the back of the angel's head.

romper:
cut 2 of white

place this line on fold of fabric

inseam

7"

9

10

11 back view

12 back view

Cherub & Lace Box

by LeNae Gerig

7" wide hexagonal papier-mâché box
¼ yard of 45" wide white lace fabric
2" tall brass cherub
2 yards of ¾" wide white ribbon with gold wired edges
2 yards of 6" wide white tulle
three ¾" wide wooden stars
gold acrylic paint
#4 flat paintbrush
twelve 1"–2" sprigs of white glittered dried baby's breath
découpage sealer (such as Mod Podge®)
gold glitter spray
low temperature glue gun and sticks·or tacky craft glue

1 Cut the lace fabric into 4"x5" rectangles. Dip them in sealer and press them to cover the inside and outside of the box and lid, overlapping only when necessary and allowing the box color to show through; let dry.

2 Cut a 20" tulle length and set the closed box in the center. Wrap the tulle around the box and lid, gluing the ends at the center top. Use the remaining tulle to make a puffy bow (see page 141) with four 3" loops and 5" tails. Glue to the lid center.

3 Use the ribbon to make a puffy bow with a center loop, twelve 2" loops and 3" tails. Glue this bow to the center of the tulle bow, then glue the cherub to the ribbon bow center.

4 Paint the stars gold and glue them to the tulle loops as shown. Glue baby's breath sprigs around the bows. Spray the lid with gold glitter.

Tulle Angel
by Marilyn Gossett

one 7½" square white battenburg doily
one 4" wide white battenburg heart doily
½ yard of white tulle net (at least 28" wide)
one 1" wide wooden ball with a ³⁄₁₆" hole
1½" length of ⅜" wooden dowel
8" length of blonde Curly Crepe™ wool hair
¼ yard of ⅜" wide gold-edged white satin ribbon
⅝ yard of ⅝" wide iridescent white flat lace
⅝ yard of 8mm gold fused pearls
five ½" wide pink ribbon roses
two 12" long stems of green silk pine with ¼" long needles
acrylic paints: light peach, black, white, mauve
paintbrushes: ¼" flat, #00 liner
black fine-tip permanent pen
tracing paper, transfer paper, pencil
pink powdered blush, cotton swab
needle, white thread
8" of gold metallic thread
low temperature glue gun and sticks or tacky craft glue

actual height 7½"

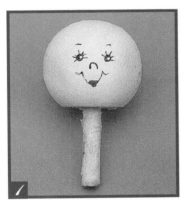

1 **Head:** Glue the dowel into the ball. Paint the ball peach; let dry. Transfer (see page 143) the face pattern and go over the lines with the pen. Paint the eyes black, the mouth mauve and the eye highlights white. Blush the cheeks.

2 **Slip:** Cut a 6½"x28" tulle piece. Sew a running stitch along one 28" edge, gather tightly around the neck and knot to secure. **Gown:** Fold down 2¼" on one edge of the square doily. Sew a running stitch along the fold and pull to gather around the neck, overlapping ½" at the back. Glue to secure. Overlap and glue the back edges together. **Arms:** Cut a 7" ribbon length, knot the center and glue the ends to the back of the neck. **Hair:** Cut into two 4" lengths and unbraid. Glue one centered on top of the head and the other behind it. Fluff and trim.

3 Form the gold thread into a loop, knot the ends together and glue the knot to the back of her neck for a hanger. **Wings:** Glue the heart doily to her back. Cut a 7½"x28" tulle piece. Sew a running stitch lengthwise down the center, gather tightly, and wrap the thread around, gluing to secure. Glue to the center back of the heart.

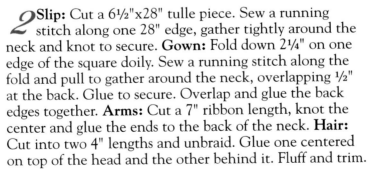

back view

4 **Halo:** Twist two pine stems together and cut to 5" long. Form into a 1¼" circle, twisting the ends to secure. Cut 10" of pearls. Wrap spiral-fashion around the wreath with the wraps ½" apart; glue the ends. Glue a rose to each side, then glue the halo to her head as shown in the large photo. **Wreath:** Make as for the halo, but form a 2" circle and wrap with 11" of pearls. Glue to her hand. Use the flat lace to make a shoestring bow (see page 141) with 2½" loops and 3" tails. Glue to the wreath top with a rose in the center.

actual width 8"

Candy Cane Angel

by Marilyn Gossett

11"x14" of navy/red calico fabric
7"x11" of polyester batting
one 1¼" wooden ball
12" of 3" wide cream gathered lace
18" of ⅛" wide red satin ribbon
one 8" long candy cane
5" of brown Curly Crepe™ wool hair
4" of ⅛" wide gold cord
12" of metallic gold thread
black fine-tip permanent pens: black, red
pink powdered blush, cotton swab
polyester fiberfill
sewing machine or needle, navy and white thread
tracing paper, transfer paper, pencil
low temperature glue gun and sticks or tacky craft glue

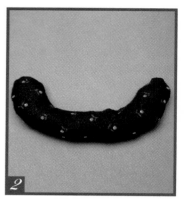

1 Trace the patterns. Cut two arms and two dress pieces from the calico. Cut one dress piece from batting. Cut two heads from muslin. **Dress:** Place the fabric pieces right sides together with the batting piece on top. Sew together with a ¼" seam, leaving a 2½" opening on the bottom. Trim the batting close to the stitching. Clip the curves and turn right side out. Sew the opening closed.

2 **Arms:** Place the fabric pieces right sides together and sew with a ¼" seam, leaving a 1½" opening on the inner curved edge. Clip curves, turn right side out and stuff firmly. Sew the opening closed.

3 Fold the dress in half along the fold line and glue the lower points together. Bend the arms around the dress top and glue to secure. Glue the hands together.

4 **Head:** Transfer (see page 143) the face to the wooden ball. Fill in the eyes and go over all the lines except the lips with black pen. Use the red pen to fill in the lips. Let dry; blush the cheeks.

   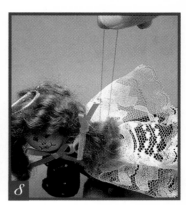

top view

5 Glue the head to the arms as shown.
Hair: Unbraid and fluff the wool hair.
Glue the center to the center top of the
head, spreading it to cover the back of the
head. Tie a 6" ribbon length around each
side of the hair, making shoestring bows (see
page 141) with ½" loops and ¾" tails. Use
the remaining ribbon to make a shoestring
bow with ¾" loops and 1" tails; glue at her
neck.

6 **Halo:** Glue the ends of the gold cord
together, overlapping them ¼". Glue
the overlapped area to the back of her hair.

7 **Wings:** Sew a running stitch along the
bound edge of the lace; gather to 1"
wide. Glue the bound edge to her back just
behind the arms. Glue the center of the lace
along the center back. Turn the cut ends
under ¼" and glue 2" down on her sides.

8 Thread the needle with gold thread and
sew a stitch through the center back ½"
from the arms. Knot the thread ends together to make a hanger. Insert the candy cane
through the arms and dress as shown in the
large photo on page 56. Adjust it to balance
the angel so she hangs straight.

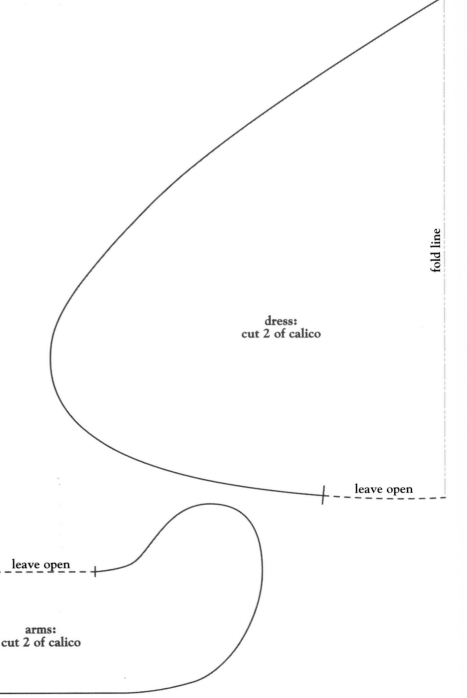

fold line

dress:
cut 2 of calico

leave open

leave open

arms:
cut 2 of calico

Sewing Angel Ornament

by Marilyn Gossett

actual width 8½"

5"x8" of 140# watercolor paper
one 1½" wide wood circle
one 3" wide acrylic heart (½ will be used)
5" of blonde Wavy Locks™ hair
½ yard of ⅛" wide blue satin ribbon
2" of ½" wide blue satin picot ribbon
4" of cream embroidery floss
round wooden toothpick
one ¾" tall wooden spool
buttons: one ⅝" blue, two ½" white
14" of 5mm gold fused pearls
9" of gold thread
fine-tip black permanent pen
acrylic paints: light peach, blue, pink, white, silver
paintbrushes: #0 liner, ½" flat
pink powdered blush
cotton swab
tracing paper, transfer paper, pencil
low temperature glue gun and sticks or tacky craft glue

right wing painting pattern

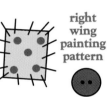

YOU ARE "SEW" SPECIAL

wings

fold line

left wing painting pattern

1. Trace the wing pattern on the fold of tracing paper and cut one from watercolor paper. Transfer (see page 143) the heart outline to the center bottom and paint the heart pink; let dry. Transfer the lettering inside the heart, the right painting pattern to the right wing and the left pattern to the left wing. Paint as shown, using the pen for black outlines, dots and stitches.

2. Cut the toothpick to 2" long, paint it silver and cut a ⅛" slit in the cut end. Glue the center of the floss into the slit. Glue the picot ribbon around the spool. Glue the spool, buttons and needle as shown, then glue the acrylic heart half over them.

3. Paint the wooden circle peach; let dry. Transfer the face and go over the lines with the pen. Blush the cheeks. Glue the head onto the wings. Fluff the hair and glue as shown.

4. Form the remaining pearls into a circle and glue for a halo. Use the ⅛" ribbon to make a shoestring bow (see page 141) with ¾" loops and 1" tails; glue at her chin. Cut the remaining ribbon in half and tie half around each side of her hair, trimming the tails to ¾". Knot the gold thread ends together, forming a loop, and glue the knot to the ornament back for a hanger.

Glove Angel Tree Topper

by Nancy Overmyer

1 size small right-handed natural cotton glove
(see page 37 to use the other glove)
½ yard of 1" wide white gathered lace
½ yard of 2½" wide white double-layered gathered lace
6" of gold metallic mini star garland
12" of 6mm ivory fused pearls
20" of strawberry blonde Mini-Curl™ curly hair
black fine-tip permanent pen
pink powdered blush, cotton swab
polyester fiberfill
needle, white thread
low temperature glue gun and sticks
   or tacky craft glue

actual height 11"

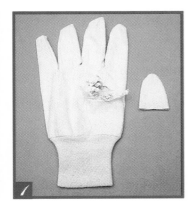

1 **Pocket:** Cut 2" off the thumb and set aside for step 3. Turn in the cut edge and glue. Cut 2" of 1" lace and glue the bound edge along the inside top of the pocket. Wind the star garland into a 1" circle and glue into the pocket behind the lace.

2 **Wings:** Pinch the two middle fingers together at the base and wrap tightly with thread so the ends fan out. Glue 1" lace around the back edge of each wing as shown.
Hands: Wrap thread tightly around each outer finger, ½" from the end. Pull the hands down and glue together.

3 **Head:** Stuff the cut-off thumb piece with fiberfill. Sew a running stitch around the cut edge, gather and knot. Cut 4½" of 1" lace and sew a running stitch along the bound edge. Gather and glue around the neck. Glue the head to the wings base. Glue ¾"–2" hair lengths over the top and sides; rub the hair between your fingers to frizz it. Use the pen to dot the eyes. Blush the cheeks.

4 Beginning at the center back, glue double lace around the glove 1" above the lower edge; cut off excess. Glue another row 1" above the first (if the glove has a cuff, glue this row along the cuff seam). Glue pearls over the bound edge of the upper lace. Form the remaining pearls into a circle and glue for her halo as shown in the large photo.

Angel in a Frame

by Marilyn Gossett

8"x10" wooden frame with 5"x7" ivory mat
one 1¼" wide wooden button
one 1¾" wide wooden heart
5"x5½" piece of posterboard
5"x5½" piece of white moiré taffeta fabric
10"x12" piece of mauve moiré taffeta fabric
paper-backed fusible web: 5"x5½" piece, 10"x12" piece
one 6" ecru crocheted doily with scallops
3 yards of white loopy yarn doll hair
acrylic paints: light peach, pink, white
1½ yards of ½" wide dusty rose braid
½ yard of ¼" wide dusty rose braid with ½" gold/white loops
½ yard of ½" wide gold/dusty rose braid
one 1" wide brass heart charm
one 1" gold wedding ring
6" of 20-gauge wire
black fine-tip permanent pen
iron, ironing board, pressing cloth
pink powdered blush, cotton swab
½" flat paintbrush
low temperature glue gun and sticks or tacky craft glue

1 Take the frame apart. Follow the manufacturer's instructions to fuse the 10"x12" web piece to the back of the mauve taffeta, then to the cardboard from the back of the frame. **Mat:** Glue rose braid along the center top and bottom, then along the center of each side as shown. Use the pen to write "~A guardian angel to watch over you~" below the top trim and "~Bless this home with love . . . ." above the bottom trim. Reassemble the frame. Glue the ends of a 12" length of rose braid to the back for a hanger.

2 Paint the wooden button and heart peach. Transfer (see page 143) the face pattern to the button and go over the features with the pen. Dip the paintbrush handle in pink paint and touch to the mouth to make a triangle of three dots. Blush the cheeks, then highlight with white dots. **Hair:** Set aside a 6" yarn length. Wrap the rest around four fingers, slip it off and tie the center with the 6" length. Glue the hair to her head and the ring for a halo.

3 **Dress:** Trace the dress pattern onto the paper backing of the remaining web piece, then fuse to the back of the white taffeta; cut out. Remove the paper and trace around it on the posterboard; cut out. Fuse the taffeta dress to the posterboard dress. Glue gold/rose braid along each side of the dress and down the center. Glue two rows of loop braid on each side as shown. Glue loop braid along the hem with the loops extending past the lower edge. Glue rose braid ½" above the hem. **Arms:** Knot an 8" length of rose braid in the center, then glue the ends to the top back.

4 (See the large photo.) **Collar:** Cut three scallops from the doily and glue the cut edge to the dress top. **Wings:** Pinch the rest of the doily in the center, wire to secure and glue to the dress top back. **Feet:** Glue the wooden heart upside down to the bottom center back of the skirt. Glue the heart charm to the hands. Glue the head to the top of the dress and the wings. Glue the angel to the frame.

dress

Shopping Angel
by Marilyn Gossett

2 5/16" tall wooden doll peg with a 7/8" wide head
4" wide cream crocheted doily
6" of 1/2" wide cream gathered lace
12" of 1/8" wide pink satin ribbon
1/8 yard of pink floral print fabric
1 3/4" of 4" wide brown twisted paper ribbon, untwisted
two 1" sprigs of bleached preserved baby's breath
two 1" sprigs of pink preserved baby's breath
one 2" wide natural cinnamay hat
five 3" lengths of strawberry blonde Mini-Curl™ curly hair
tracing paper, transfer paper, pencil
acrylic paints: black, white
#00 liner brush
1" ball of polyester fiberfill
pink powdered blush, cotton swab
needle and thread or sewing machine
6" of 24-gauge wire
low temperature glue gun and sticks or tacky craft glue

actual height 6"

1 Transfer (see page 143) the face pattern to the peg. Paint the features and stitching lines black. Blush the cheeks.

2 **Dress:** Cut a 4½"x11" fabric piece and sew a running stitch ⅛" from one long edge. Gather around the neck, knot to secure and glue in place. Glue the ½" lace for a collar. **Arms:** Cut a 2"x8" fabric piece. Fold in ½" on each long edge, then fold in half lengthwise, wrong sides together. Knot 1" from each end. Glue the center to the upper back of the doll. Bring the hands to the front and glue together as shown in the large photo.

3 Glue the hair to the head. Glue the hat to the hair. Fold up the brim front and glue to secure. Glue the baby's breath between the brim and the crown. Use 6" of ribbon to make a shoestring bow (see page 141) with ½" loops and ¾" tails. Glue it to the brim front.

4 **Wings:** Pinch the doily center and wire to secure. Glue to her back. **Shopping bag:** Fold the paper ribbon to measure 1¾"x2" and glue the sides. Fill it with the fiberfill, pinch the top together and glue. Glue the bag into her arms as shown in the large photo. Knot the ends of the remaining ribbon together, forming a loop, and glue to her upper back for a hanger.

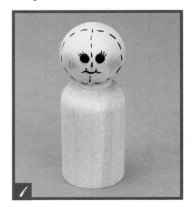

Quick & Easy Gifts

It's always fun to receive a hand-crafted gift from someone—it makes you feel so special! In this section we've provided a wide variety of gifts, something for nearly everyone in your life. Items such as jewelry, painted shirts, beautifully decorated bottles, candles and decorations for the home are included.

Some are elegant, such as the Magnolia Box, the Battenburg Wall Decorations and the Gold Pomegranate Bottle. The Funny Bunting Bunny is a soft, fun toy for that special little one. There are also cute gifts such as the Duck Dot Shirt, the Sewing Doll and the Scarecrow Pin.

You could even carry the "handmade" theme further by making your own unique wrapping paper. Dip a sponge shape into paint and press it randomly onto white paper for a quick and easy, festive wrap-up. Add an ornament or a sprig of pine to the bow to complete it and you have a wonderful gift for a very special friend or loved one!

If you make a papier-mâché box as a gift, tuck in some homemade cookies, potpourri, jewelry or peppermint candies to make it extra special. A beautifully decorated bottle could contain scented oil or bath beads for a personal gift. Or use the same types of materials to decorate both a box and a bottle, making a coordinating set.

All these gifts are easy to make, yet look like you've spent hours creating each one. And because of the variety, you should find something for everyone on your Christmas list!

Kitty Earrings

by Lori Thompson

for each pair:
ruler
round wooden toothpick
baking dish, oven
wire cutters, needlenose or jewelry pliers

for the black cats:
polymer clay (see page 143): black, green, white
two 4mm black beads
2 silver eye pins
2 silver fishhook earwires

for the white cats:
polymer clay (see page 143): white, green, red
2 gold eye pins
2 gold fishhook earwires

actual height of each cat 1½"

○ 1/16"   ○ 1/8"   ◯ 1/4"   ◯ 1/2"   leaf   rosebud

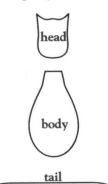

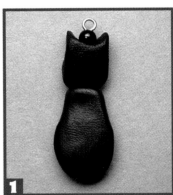

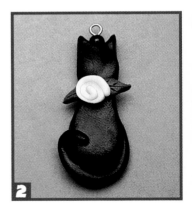

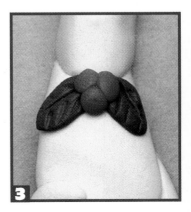

1 **Black cat earrings:** Roll a ¼" ball of black clay. Flatten with your forefinger and pinch up two ears. Roll a ½" ball and flatten to match the body pattern; attach the head at the top. Cut an eye pin to 1" long and insert through a bead, then through the head into the body.

2 Roll a ⅛"x1¼" black rope and attach for a tail, curving it around the body as shown. Flatten two ⅛" green balls to match the leaf pattern; use a toothpick to draw vein lines. Attach to the neck, points outward. Roll a ⅛"x½" white rope and flatten slightly, then roll into a spiral rosebud. Attach to the leaf centers. Repeat steps 1–2 for the second earring, curving the tail in the opposite direction. Bake at 250° for 30 minutes; cool completely before removing. Use the pliers to open the eye of an earwire, hook it through an eye pin and close. Repeat for the other earring.

3 **White cat earrings:** Follow steps 1–2, using white clay in place of black. Omit the beads and rosebuds. Roll six 1/16" red clay balls for berries. Attach three to each cat over the leaf centers.

Hearts & Roses Earrings

by Lori Thompson

polymer clay (see page 143): white, green,
   pink
2 gold eye pins
2 gold fishhook earwires
1¼" wide heart cutter (or cut with a knife
   using the pattern below)
rolling pin
ruler
round wooden toothpick
baking dish, oven
wire cutters, needlenose or jewelry pliers

actual height of each heart 1¼"

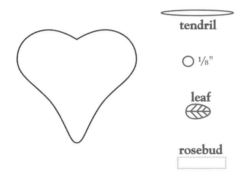

tendril

○ ⅛"

leaf

rosebud

1 Roll white clay to ⅛" thick and cut two hearts. Smooth the rough edges and round the points.

2 Cut the eye pins to 1" long and insert one into the top of each heart. Use the tip of a toothpick to imprint the dot pattern around each heart.

3 Flatten four ⅛" green balls to match the leaf pattern; use a toothpick to draw vein lines. Attach two to each heart as shown. Roll four 1/16"x¾" green ropes and coil each around a toothpick to form a tendril. Attach two to each heart as shown.

4 Roll a ⅛"x½" pink rope and flatten slightly, then roll up to form a rosebud; repeat for three more rosebuds. Attach two to each heart over the tops of the tendrils. Roll six ⅛" pink balls and imprint an X in the top of each. Attach three to each heart among the tendrils. Bake at 250° for 30 minutes; cool completely before removing. Use the pliers to open the eye of an earwire, hook it through an eye pin and close. Repeat for the other earring.

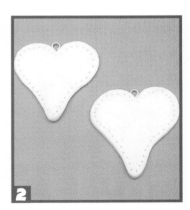

Earring Tote

by Arlene Anderson

4½"x9" piece of purple/mauve double-faced quilted fabric
two 2"x5" pieces of mauve broadcloth fabric
4½" of 1" wide cream gathered lace
3" of ⅛" wide mauve satin ribbon
1" of ¾" wide hook-and-loop tape (Velcro®)
3" square of 7-mesh plastic canvas
sewing machine, matching thread, straight pins

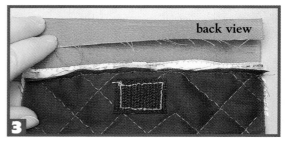

1 Separate the hook and loop sides of the fastener tape and sew one piece at each 4½" end of the quilted fabric, centering it on the wrong side ½" from the edge.

2 Pin the lace to the wrong side of one end, placing its bound edge even with the raw edge. Fold the ribbon in half and pin the cut ends even with the raw edge.

3 Pin a fabric strip over the lace and ribbon with one long edge even with the raw edge. Sew ¼" from the raw edge through all the layers. Press the fabric strip upward, then press ½" of the other long edge to the wrong side.

4 Fold the pressed edge down and pin it in place just overlapping the previous stitching line. Turn the tote right side up as shown. Sew close to the lower edge of the binding, catching the back edge in the stitching. Repeat steps 3–4 to bind the other end, omitting the lace and ribbon.

5 Fold the tote in half, right sides together. Trim the binding ends even. Sew ¼" from each side, top to bottom. Turn right side out, press and insert the plastic canvas. Press the fastener pieces together to close the tote.

School Days Tote

by Arlene Anderson

10"x24" piece of green medium-weight fabric
8"x10" piece of print fabric
½ yard of ⅝" wide striped grosgrain ribbon
ruler, chalk
sewing machine, matching thread, straight pins, iron

to fill the tote:
8-count box of crayons
3 pencils
3"x5" notepad

1 Fold the green fabric in half crosswise so it measures 10"x12"; press the fold. Chalk a line parallel to the fold, 1¼" away. **Pocket:** Fold the print fabric in half lengthwise so it measures 4"x10"; press the fold. Open the green fabric flat and pin the raw edges of the print piece on the chalk line with the pocket extending downward, across the fold of the green fabric. Sew ¼" from the raw edge of the pocket. Fold the pocket upward and press in place.

2 Measure and chalk a line 4½" from each end of the pocket, parallel to the raw edges. Sew along these lines, forming a 1" center pocket.

3 Fold the tote in half crosswise, right sides together, and sew ½" from each side. Turn right side out and press. The pocket should now begin 1" above the bottom of the bag; it should have a center pocket and two 4" side pockets.

4 **Top hem:** Fold the upper edge ½" to the inside; press; repeat. **Handles:** Cut the ribbon into two 9" lengths. Insert one end of one piece into the hem 2¼" from the side seam. Repeat with the other end on the other side. Fold the ribbon upward and pin to secure. Repeat on the other side of the bag. Sew around the hem close to the folded edge, catching the ribbon. Repeat ¼" away. Fill the tote with the crayons, notepad and pencils as shown in the large photo.

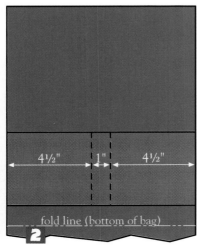

fold line (bottom of bag)

4½" 1" 4½"

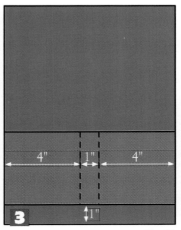

4" 1" 4"

1"

Sponge-Painted Apron

by LeNae Gerig

19"x27" unbleached canvas apron with pockets
4"x7" piece of compressed sponge
black fine-tip permanent pen
fabric paints: golden yellow, red, brown, black
white dimensional paint
ruler, soft pencil, masking tape
scissors
paper plate, paper towels

1" square

1 Use the ruler and pencil to mark five 1" wide stripes across the apron top and two along the top of the pockets. Trace the gingerbread boy, star and 1" square patterns, cut out, then cut from the sponge. Moisten with water to expand; squeeze out excess water. Pour a puddle of red paint into a paper plate. Dip the square sponge into the paint, dab off excess on a paper towel, and press onto the apron, making a checkerboard of squares 1" apart between the marked lines. Let dry.

2 Pour a puddle of brown paint into the plate. Sponge a gingerbread boy into the center top of the apron over the checkerboard. Sponge half a gingerbread boy extending out of the right pocket. Sponge three yellow stars as shown.

3 Dip the eraser end of the pencil into black paint and dot the eyes and mouth on each gingerbread boy. Clean the eraser and dip into red paint to dot the cheeks and buttons. Squiggle dimensional paint cuffs and hair on each boy as shown.

4 Use the black pen to outline each star and gingerbread boy, then make crosswise stitches as shown on the outlines. Draw turned-up corners on each mouth.

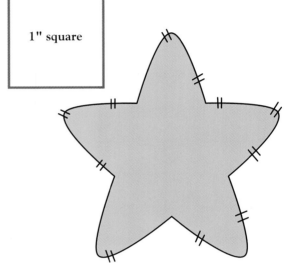

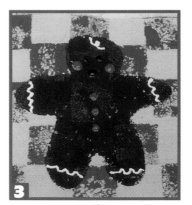

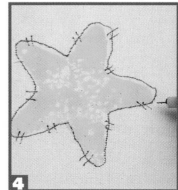

Funny Bunting Bunny

by Annie Cullie

two 8"x10" pieces of white bunting or heavy brushed knit fabric
1"x2" of pink felt
pom poms: one 7mm pink, two 3mm black, two 10mm white,
   one 1" white
12" of ⅜" wide light green satin ribbon
12" of 6-strand pink embroidery floss
embroidery needle, sewing machine, white thread
polyester fiberfill, tracing paper, pencil, scissors
low temperature glue gun and sticks or tacky craft glue

actual height 7½"

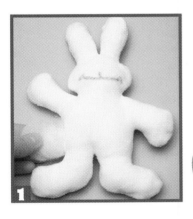

1 Trace the patterns. Transfer (see page 143) the bunny pattern onto the **wrong** side of one piece of white fabric. On the right side, embroider the mouth with chain stitch (see right). Place the two pieces right sides together and sew along the line, leaving an opening at one side. Sew again over the first stitching for strength. Trim the fabric to within ¼" of the stitching, clip the curves and turn right side out. Stuff, using the eraser end of the pencil to push stuffing into the corners. Sew the opening closed.

chain stitch

French knot

2 Cut the paw pads from pink felt; glue as shown. Glue the white pom poms above the mouth for a muzzle, the pink pom pom for a nose, and the black pom poms for eyes.

3 Split the embroidery floss and use three strands for the navel. Knot one end of the floss, insert from back to front through the body, and pull tight. Make a French knot (see at right); repeat twice. Insert the needle back through the body, knot at the back, and cut the thread. Glue the white pom pom for his tail. Tie the ribbon around his neck in a shoestring bow (see page 141) with 1" loops and 1½" tails.

Country Cutie Pins
by Jackie Zars

girl's height 2"; scarecrow's height 2½"

for each pin:
one 1" wide wooden button
one 2" wide straw hat (½ will be used for each)
one ¾" long pin back
acrylic paints: black, white, terra cotta
paintbrushes: #2 round, #00 liner
tracing paper, transfer paper, pencil
low temperature glue gun and sticks or tacky craft glue

for the girl:
3" of light brown Whimsey™ Hair
1¼" of ½" wide white flat lace
9" of ⅛" wide mauve satin ribbon
one ⅜" wide blue ribbon rose
acrylic paints: light peach, brown, pink
matte acrylic varnish

for the scarecrow:
2" square of unbleached muslin fabric
½"x4" strip of blue print fabric
eight 2" lengths of raffia

1 **Girl:** Paint the button peach. Transfer (see page 143) the face pattern. Paint the eyes and eyelashes black and the mouth brown. Dot white highlights in the eyes and at the eye corners. Dilute terra cotta paint with an equal amount of water and blush her cheeks. Let dry; varnish.

2 Glue on her hair; fluff and trim it around her face. Cut the hat in half and glue it to her hair. Glue the ribbon rose to the crown as shown. Referring to the large photo, glue lace to the bottom back of the button for her collar. Use the ribbon to tie a shoestring bow (see page 141) with ½" loops and 1¼" tails; glue to the collar front. Glue on the pin back.

3 **Scarecrow:** Glue muslin to cover the button, leaving one unglued side extending downward. Transfer the face pattern. Paint the eyes, eyebrows, eyelashes, mouth and stitches black. Paint the nose terra cotta. Blot excess paint off on a paper towel and use the nearly dry brush to lightly paint his cheeks terra cotta.

4 Tie the print strip around his neck for a scarf. Tie one raffia length around the others, then glue the knot to the head top, arranging the strands to form hair. Cut the hat in half and glue over the hair as shown in the large photo. Glue on the pin back.

Little Seamstress

by Jackie Zars

one 3½" long wooden pear
one 1½" long wooden ball knob
wooden thread spools: one ⅜" tall, one ¾" tall
3" square of sewing pattern tissue
embroidery floss: burgundy, pink
5½"x12" piece of blue print calico fabric
¼ yard of 1¾" wide ivory gathered lace
4" of 1" wide ivory gathered lace
acrylic paints: light peach, coral, white, black, light blue
paintbrushes: ½" flat, #0 round
1" of 20-gauge wire
6" of ⅛" wide ivory satin ribbon
one ⅜" wide pink button
blonde Mini Curl™ curly hair
needle, blue thread
tracing paper, transfer paper, pencil
low temperature glue gun and sticks
   or tacky craft glue

actual height 5½"

1 Glue the 1¾" lace around the pear 1¾" above the bottom; overlap ½" at the back and trim excess.
Dress: Tear a 3½"x12" fabric strip. Sew a running stitch ¼" from one long edge, pull to gather, and glue around the pear top. Glue the back edges together. Glue the 1" lace around the dress top.

2 **Sleeves:** Tear a 2"x9½" fabric strip and fold the long edges in to make a 1" wide strip. Glue the center to the dress top back, raw edges toward the dress. Bring the sleeves together in front and wire 1" from the ends, forming "hands." Use the ribbon to make a shoestring bow (see page 141) with 1" loops and 1" tails. Glue the bow to the hands; glue the button to the bow center.

3 **Head:** Paint the ball peach; let dry. Transfer (see page 143) the face pattern. Paint the eyes white, the irises blue, and the pupils, mouth, eyelashes and outlines black. Dot a white highlight in each eye. Dilute coral paint with an equal amount of water and blush the cheeks. Glue the head to the top of the pear.

4 **Hair:** Cut three 3" hair lengths. Glue the center of each length to the center of the head, working from front to back. Rub the hair between your fingers to frizz it. Fluff and trim it to cover the head. Tear a 4"x½" fabric strip and knot it at the center; trim the ends to 1" long. Glue the knot to the center top of her head. **Finishing:** Wrap the small spool with burgundy floss and the large spool with pink floss. Glue the spools and the pattern piece into her arms as shown in the large photo above.

Raffia Doll

by Marilyn Gossett

4 oz. of glycerine-preserved raffia
12½"x20" piece of green/cream striped fabric
¾ yard of 1" wide white gathered crocheted lace
18" of ⅞" wide light pink satin picot ribbon
eight ⅜" wide light pink ribbon rosebuds
two 5" long heads of dried wheat
one 1" wide wooden ball
needle, ivory thread
acrylic paints: pink, cream
water-based acrylic sealer
#8 flat paintbrush
low temperature glue gun and sticks or tacky craft glue

1 Body: Trim the raffia strands to 36" long (save the trimmings for tying strands and hair). Tie the center of the bundle with a single raffia strand. Wrap the bundle around the wooden ball with the knot on the inside. Arrange the strands to cover the ball; glue to secure. Pull out a single strand and wrap it tightly under the ball, forming a neck. Tie this strand into a 3" hanging loop as shown, then trim off the end. Trim the rest of the raffia ends to 11" and divide into three equal bunches. **Arms:** Divide each outer bunch into thirds, braid for 4", then tie below the braid with a single strand. Trim the tails to 3".

2 Hands: Fold the strands up on the end of each arm. Tie at the wrist and trim excess. **Hair:** Trim the remaining raffia strands to 10"; wrap and tie at one end. Braid for 5" and tie below the braid. Trim off the tails. Glue the braid around the head, overlapping the ends at the bottom back. Glue a rosebud on each side.

3 Dress: Cut a 7½"x20" fabric piece and glue lace along one long edge; trim excess. Sew a running stitch ¼" from the other long edge and pull to gather it around the body under the arms. Overlap the short edges in back and glue the dress in place. Tie the ribbon around the waist, making a shoestring bow with 1" loops and 3" tails.

4 Sleeves: Cut a 5"x6½" fabric piece and fold in half lengthwise. Sew or glue in a ¼" seam. Wrong side out, slip the sleeve end over one hand and turn so the seam is next to the body. Wrap tightly over the wrist with thread and knot. Turn the sleeve right side out, pulling it up to the shoulder. Fold the raw edges in and glue to the shoulder. Repeat for the other sleeve, forming a V-shaped neckline. Cut 7" of lace, turn the bound edge under and glue for a collar. Glue a rosebud to the center front. Glue the remaining rosebuds around the hem as shown in the large photo. Hold the hands together and insert the wheat stems through the loops; glue to secure.

actual height 13"

Heart Garland

by Kathy Thompson

Materials:

12"x5" piece of burgundy/green paisley print fabric
6"x5" piece of burgundy/rose print fabric
5"x18" piece of fusible interfacing, iron
1½ yards of 1" wide white gathered lace
12" of ⅛" wide ivory satin ribbon
32" of 1/16" wide dark pink satin ribbon
1 yard of ⅜" wide dusty rose satin ribbon
four ¾" wide burgundy ribbon roses
¼ oz. of preserved plumosus
¼ oz. of bleached dried baby's breath
polyester fiberfill
tracing paper, pencil
low temperature glue gun and sticks or tacky craft glue

1 Trace the heart pattern; cut out. Iron interfacing onto the back of each fabric piece. Cut out four paisley hearts and two burgundy hearts. Place the hearts together in like pairs, wrong sides together, and glue each pair around the edge, leaving a 2" opening at one side. Stuff softly and glue the openings closed.

2 Cut three 18" lace lengths. Beginning at the center top, glue one around each heart.

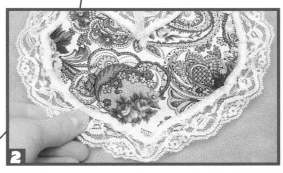

3 Glue the hearts side by side, overlapping ¼", to form a curve as shown in the large photo. Cut a 6" length of ⅛" ribbon, fold in half and glue the ends to the one end of the garland. Repeat on the other end.

4 Cut four 9" lengths of ⅜" ribbon. Use each to make a shoestring bow (see page 141) with 1" loops and 1½" tails. Glue one over the ends of each ⅛" ribbon loop. Glue one to each side of the center heart where it overlaps a paisley heart. Cut four 8" lengths of 1/16" ribbon and use each to tie a shoestring bow with ¾" loops and 1¼" tails. Glue one to the center of each ⅜" ribbon bow. Glue a rose to the center of each bow. Cut 1"–1½" sprigs of baby's breath and plumosus; glue evenly spaced around the roses.

Peach Heart Box

by Randa Black

one 3¼"x1½" papier-mâché heart box
peach acrylic paint, #8 flat paintbrush
one 2" wide white heart doily
peach ribbon roses: one 1" wide, two ½" wide
two ½" wide peach butterfly buttons
two ½" wide pearl-centered gold buttons
⅓ yard of ½" wide white satin gimp braid
⅓ yard of 3.5mm white fused pearls
⅓ yard of 1/16" wide peach satin ribbon
⅓ yard of 1/16" wide cream satin ribbon
gold glitter mist spray, old newspapers
low temperature glue gun and sticks or tacky
   craft glue

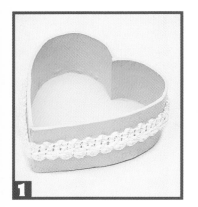

1 Paint the box inside and out with one heavy coat of peach paint; repeat for the lid; let dry. Glue the gimp braid around the box bottom as shown.

2 Glue the doily to lid top center. Glue pearls around the rim of the lid.

3 Glue the 1" rose to the top center of the doily center. Glue a ¼" rose above left of it and one below right. Glue the butterflies and buttons evenly spaced onto the design. Hold both ribbons together and handle as one to tie a shoestring bow (see page 141) with 1" loops and 3" tails. Glue the bow below left of the 1" rose. Place the box and lid on newspapers and mist with gold glitter mist; let dry; repeat.

Woodlands Box

by LeNae Gerig

7¾" round papier-mâché box
walnut woodtone spray stain
dark brown acrylic paint
#10 round paintbrush
woodgraining tool —————————
5 oz. of 1" long pine cones
2" long pink/blue mushroom bird
2 oz. of sheet moss
six 1"–2" clusters of natural canella berries
½ oz. of green preserved sprengeri
1 pink silk dogwood stem with two 2" sprigs and
     one 5" sprig, each with a 3" wide blossom
1 artificial raspberry stem with eight clusters of
     two and three ½" wide berries and many 1¾"
     long leaves
four 46" long raffia strands
low temperature glue gun and sticks or tacky
     craft glue

1 Spray the inside and outside of the box with stain; let dry. Use the brush to paint the outside of the box brown. While the paint is still wet scrape with the graining tool, texturing it to resemble wood. Let dry.

2 Glue moss to cover the lid. Working from the edge to the center, glue the cones close together to cover the moss. Wrap the raffia around the lid and tie in a shoestring bow (see page 141) with 2" loops and 4" tails. Glue the bow to the lid front center. Cut the sprigs from the dogwood stem; glue the 2" long sprigs to the back left and the 5" sprig curving between them to the right as shown.

3 Cut the berry stem into four 3", one 5" and two 7" sprigs. Glue the 5" sprig to the left side of the lid, one 7" sprig between the 2" dogwood sprigs, and the other 7" sprig extending right from behind the 5" dogwood sprig. Glue the remaining 3" sprigs around the 2" dogwood sprigs and to the right of the 5" berry sprig.

4 Glue 1" moss tufts and the canella clusters around the berries and blossoms. Fill empty spaces with 2"–3" sprigs of sprengeri. Glue the bird to the center.

Heart Hanging

by Randa Black

one 6" ecru stiffened crocheted doily heart
one 5" square of burgundy moiré fabric
1 ⅓ yards of ¼" wide gold metallic ribbon
one 2½" long gold tassel
four ½" wide dark pink satin ribbon roses
two ½" wide cream satin ribbon roses
gold "I Love You" charms: one 1¼" wide, one ½" wide
one ¾" long gold rose charm
tracing paper, pencil, 4" square of posterboard
tacky craft glue

1 Transfer (see page 143) the heart pattern onto the poster-board; cut out. Cover the posterboard with a thin layer of tacky glue. Center the fabric on the posterboard and press gently into place; let dry. Trim the fabric ¼" larger than the posterboard. Pull the edges to the back, clipping as needed, and glue to secure.

2 Cut one 24", one 18" and one 6" ribbon length. Beginning at the bottom, weave the 24" length through the outer holes of the heart. Knot the ends, trim to ¼" and glue to the heart back. Repeat with 18" length around the inner holes.

3 Glue the covered heart to the wreath back. Glue the ends of the 6" ribbon length to the top back for a hanger. Knot ½" from the tassel top, cut off above the knot and glue the knot to the bottom back. Glue the charms and roses as shown.

Mothers' Wreath

by Randa Black

one 4" wide ecru stiffened crocheted doily wreath
one 3½" square of burgundy moiré taffeta fabric
three ½" wide mauve satin ribbon roses with leaves
three ½" wide cream satin ribbon roses with leaves
one 2½" long mauve tassel
28" of ⅛" wide gold metallic ribbon
one 2"x¾" gold "Mother" charm
one 1½" wide gold bow charm
one 2½" circle of posterboard, tacky craft glue

2½" circle

1 Cover the posterboard with a thin layer of glue. Center the fabric on the posterboard and press gently into place; let dry. Trim the fabric ¼" larger than the posterboard, pull the edges to the back and glue to secure. Glue to the wreath back.

2 Cut one 12", one 10" and one 6" ribbon length. Use the 6" length to form a hanging loop; glue the ends to the top back. Weave the 10" length through the inner wreath holes, knot the ends in the back and glue to secure. Repeat with the 12" length through the outer holes.

3 Knot ½" from the tassel top, cut off above the knot and glue the knot to the bottom back. Glue the charms and roses as shown.

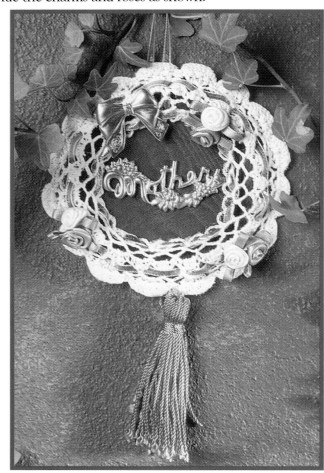

Doily Heart

by LeNae Gerig

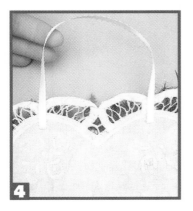

one 7" wide battenburg heart doily
ten ⅞" wide burgundy ribbon
     roses
nine ½" wide mauve ribbon roses
1¼ yard of ⅜" wide white satin
     picot ribbon
2 yards of ⅛" wide white satin
     ribbon
1 yard of ¼" wide burgundy satin
     ribbon
¼ oz. of preserved plumosus
1 oz. of white dried German
     statice
¼ oz. of bleached dried baby's
     breath
fabric stiffener, waxed paper
tacky craft glue
low temperature glue gun and
     sticks

1 Follow the manufacturer's instructions to stiffen the doily; let dry overnight on waxed paper. Cut the plumosus into 2"–3" sprigs. Use tacky glue to attach them to the doily as shown. Let dry.

2 Cut 36" of the picot ribbon. Loop and glue among the plumosus sprigs, twisting and gluing the ribbon every 2". Glue the burgundy roses evenly spaced around the doily as shown.

3 Glue mauve roses between the burgundy roses. Cut the statice and baby's breath into 1"–2" sprigs and glue among the roses.

4 Glue the ends of the remaining picot ribbon to the back shoulders of the heart, forming a hanger. Cut the ⅛" ribbon into two 1-yard lengths. Hold together with the burgundy ribbon to make a shoestring bow (see page 141) with 1½" loops and 16" tails. Knot each tail ½" from the end. Glue the bow to the center top of the heart as shown in the large photo.

Jute Bottle

by Marilyn Gossett

*one 12½" tall green glass bottle
   with a cork
6 yards of 3-ply jute twine
eight 36" long strands of raffia
one Christmas pick with one 2"
   long pine cone, three 2" long
   pine sprigs, three 2" long holly
   leaves and a cluster of eight ½"
   wide gold berries
seven 3" sprigs of white dried
   German statice
low temperature glue gun and sticks
   or tacky craft glue*

1 Cut a 24" length of jute. Apply glue to the top of the cork. Fold under ½" on one end of the jute and attach to the center of the cork. Coil it around the top and sides as shown, adding glue as needed; leave ¼" of the cork Punwrapped. Insert the cork into the bottle.

2 Glue one end of the remaining jute to the middle of the bottle. Wrap in tight coils, spot-gluing as needed to secure. Trim excess.

3 Hold the raffia lengths together and tie around the bottle neck in a shoestring bow (see page 141) with 3" loops and 9" tails. Cut the stem off the pick. Glue the pick to the bow center, then glue statice around the bow as shown in the large photo.

Pomegranate Bottle

by Marilyn Gossett

one 11½" tall glass pyramid bottle with a cork
1 yard of ¼" wide metallic gold trim
one 1" wide wood button
three 36" long raffia strands
1 pick with three 1" wide purple pomegranates
    and 1½"–3" long stems
six 3" long sprigs of green preserved eucalyptus
¼ oz. of Spanish moss
metallic gold spray enamel
matte acrylic spray sealer
9" of 30-gauge wire, wire cutters
low temperature glue gun and sticks or tacky
    craft glue

1 Glue the button to the cork top; place the cork in the bottle. Spray the entire bottle gold; let dry. Spray with sealer; let dry. Pull and twist the moss into a 9" length and glue around the bottle neck as shown.

2 Cut the stem off the pick. Wrap the wire tightly around the bottoms of the pomegranate stems, then wrap around the bottle neck over the moss; trim excess wire. Glue the eucalyptus around the pomegranates, extending outward as shown.

3 Hold the raffia strands together and tie in a shoestring bow (see page 141) with 2" loops and 6" tails. Glue above the pomegranates. Use your thumbnail to split and shred the loops and tails. Use the trim to make a loopy bow (see page 140) with six 1"–1½" loops and 6" tails. Glue to the raffia bow center as shown in the large photo.

Toy Soldier

by Marilyn Gossett

one 4½" tall square glass bottle
one 1½" wide wooden ball knob
one 1½" tall wooden candle cup
red and black jellybeans
acrylic paints: black, metallic gold, red, white, light peach,
   blue, brown, coral
paintbrushes: #4 flat, #0 liner
black fine-tip permanent pen
⅓ yard of ⅛" wide gold metallic braid trim
gloss acrylic sealer
round wooden toothpick
low temperature glue gun and sticks or tacky craft glue

actual height 7½"

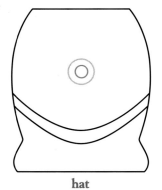

hat

1 **Head:** Paint the knob peach. Transfer (see page 143) the face pattern. Paint the cheeks coral. Outline the features with the pen. Paint the hair brown. Dip the paintbrush handle into blue paint and touch to the eye positions to make dots. Repeat to make smaller black dots for pupils, then dip the toothpick in white to dot highlights.

2 **Hat:** Turn the candle cup upside down. Paint it black, then paint a white stripe curving across the front. Make a gold dot in the center front, then a smaller red dot in the center of the gold one.

3 Glue the head onto the cork. Glue the hat onto the head. Seal; let dry. Dot five gold buttons down the top front of the bottle. Tie the braid around the neck in a shoestring bow (see page 141) with 1" loops and 1½" tails. Fill the bottom half of the bottle with black jellybeans (for his pants) and the top with red jellybeans. Replace the cork.

Rose Candle

by LeNae Gerig

one 3"x6" burgundy pillar
  candle
1 burgundy silk rosebud stem
  with a 1" wide blossom
  and 6 green leaves
1 yard of 1⅜" wide gold
  wire-edged mesh ribbon
matte acrylic spray sealer
gold glitter spray
low temperature glue gun and
  sticks or tacky craft glue

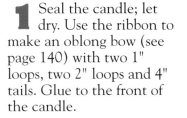

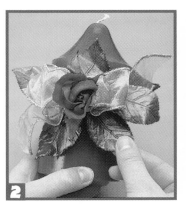

1 Seal the candle; let dry. Use the ribbon to make an oblong bow (see page 140) with two 1" loops, two 2" loops and 4" tails. Glue to the front of the candle.

2 Cut the rosebud and leaves from the stem. Glue the bud to the bow center. Curve the leaves into natural shapes and glue among the bow loops.

3 Spray the entire project with glitter spray; let dry. **Note:** This candle is for decorative use only—do not burn it.

Dot Appliqué Techniques

basic supplies:
- dimensional paints
- black pen
- shirt board or plastic-covered cardboard
- waxed paper
- white paper
- straight pins
- ruler
- fabric glue

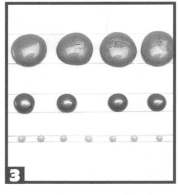
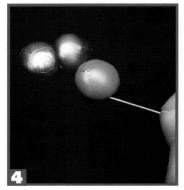

1 Use the ruler and pen to draw two parallel lines ½" apart on the white paper. Repeat to make line pairs ⅜" apart, ¼", ³⁄₁₆", ⅛" and ¹⁄₁₆". These will be your guides for squeezing dots. Lay a sheet of waxed paper over the ruled lines.

2 Shake the paint into the bottle tip (it helps to store the bottle upside down). Squeeze the bottle, applying gentle pressure until the dot grows to the needed size.

3 Referring to the project instructions, squeeze the required colors and sizes of dots onto the waxed paper. Let them dry overnight.

4 Insert the shirt board into the shirt to protect it from excess glue. **Applying the dots:** Use a straight pin to pick the dot off the waxed paper.

Squeeze a dot of fabric glue onto the garment where the dot will go, then place the paint dot in the glue. (Dots will stick to each other, so glue is not needed when applying dots over other dots.)

String of Pearls Shirt

by Mary Carroll

black t-shirt
pearlescent dimensional paint dots:
    lavender—nine ½",
      twenty-four ⅛"
    gold—nine ½",
      twenty-five ⅛",
      twenty-three ¹⁄₁₆"
    green—nine ½",
      twenty-three ¼",
      twenty-five ⅛"
    red—nine ½",
      twenty-six ⅛"
    blue—nine ½"
basic supplies (see above)

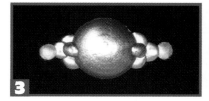

1 Arrange the ½" dots on the shirt, overlapping them ⅛" and forming a zig-zag chain. When you are satisfied with the arrangement, lift off one dot at a time and glue in place.

2 Position and glue the other dots as shown.

3 With the remaining dots, make a small pattern on the right sleeve as shown.

Ducky Dot Shirt

by Mary Carroll

red t-shirt
shiny dimensional paint dots:
  yellow—eighteen ½",
    eighteen ⅜",
    six ¼",
    twenty-six ⅛"
  orange—ten ³⁄₁₆",
    seventeen ⅛"
  black—one ½",
    one ⅜"
  white—one ⅛",
    two ¹⁄₁₆"
basic supplies (see page 82)

1 **For each duck:** Use a ½" dot for the body, a ⅛" dot for the neck and a ⅜" dot for the head. Cut a ⅛" orange dot in half and glue edgewise for the feet.

2 Referring to the large photo, position and glue fourteen yellow ducks and one black duck across the shirt chest. Press on ¹⁄₁₆" black dots for eyes and ³⁄₁₆" orange dots for beaks.

3 Arrange the remaining yellow in groups of six dots of descending sizes. Glue a set of dots at each end of the row of ducks, trailing outward from large to small. Glue the last set of dots, large dot at the top, to the right sleeve as shown in the large photo.

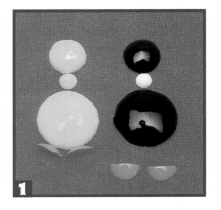

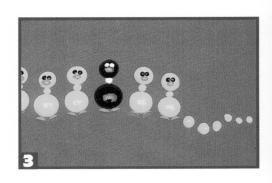

Doily Sachet by Francie Dunwell

one 6" square lace-edged white fabric doily
one 1" wide pink/yellow dried rosebud
five 2" long sprigs of green preserved eucalyptus
five 2" sprigs of white dried German statice
1–2 tablespoons of potpourri
2" tuft of Spanish moss
4" of 1/8" wide white satin ribbon
1 yard of 1/16" wide dusty rose satin ribbon
small handful of polyester fiberfill
low temperature glue gun and sticks or tacky craft glue

1 Place the doily face down and center the fiberfill on it; place the potpourri on top. Fold the doily in half, forming a triangle. Glue the sides together along the inner edge of the lace.

2 Fold the top doily tip down and glue to secure. Glue moss over the fold. Glue the rosebud into the moss, then glue the eucalyptus sprigs evenly spaced around it. Glue the statice sprigs between the eucalyptus sprigs.

3 Use the rose ribbon to make a loopy bow (see page 140) with eight 2" loops and 4" tails. Glue at the bottom right of the moss as shown in the large photo. Knot and glue the ends of the white ribbon to the top back as shown, forming a hanger.

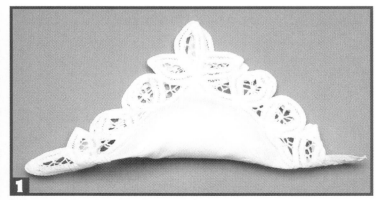

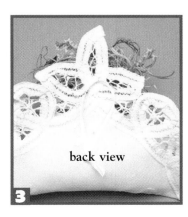

back view

Hanging Bouquet

by Francie Dunwell

one 8″ square lace-edged white fabric doily
four 1″ long pink dried rosebuds
½ oz. of green preserved boxwood
½ oz. of white dried German statice
¼ oz. of pink dried rice grass
4″ of ⅛″ wide white satin ribbon
½ yard of ⅝″ wide dark pink satin ribbon
1″x1″x4″ block of floral foam for dried flowers
low temperature glue gun and sticks or tacky craft glue

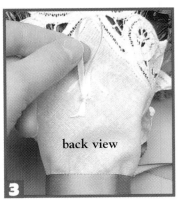

back view

1 Cut two 8″ boxwood sprigs and insert into the top of the foam. Cut two 4″ sprigs; insert towards the front of the foam, angling slightly forward. Insert the rosebuds so the center back one extends 7″, the center front rosebud extends 4″ and angles slightly forward, one extends 6″ and angles left, and the last extends 5″ and angles right.

2 Cut the statice and rice grass into 2″–8″ sprigs; insert near boxwood and rosebud sprigs of similar heights. Fill any empty spaces with boxwood sprigs. Lay the bouquet diagonally on the doily.

3 Wrap the doily around, overlapping it in front, to form a cone. Glue to secure. Wrap the pink ribbon around the center of the cone and tie in a shoestring bow (see page 141) with 2″ loops and 5″ tails. Knot and glue the ends of the white ribbon to the top back as shown, forming a hanger.

Santa on a Shirt

by Linda Patterson

1 white t-shirt
shirt board or plastic-covered cardboard
straight pins
tracing paper, transfer paper, pencil
fabric paints: white, light peach, pink, pearlescent
*   green, pearlescent red*
dimensional paints: white, clear
*   iridescent glitter*
fabric paintbrushes: ¼" wide, #00 liner
round wooden toothpick
old toothbrush
2"x4" paper scrap
black fine-tip permanent pen

1 Place the shirt on the shirt board and secure it with pins—the fabric should be taut, but not stretched. Transfer (see page 143) the pattern to the left chest area. Paint the shoes black, the suit and hat red, the mittens green, the face peach, and the hair, eyebrows, beard, mustache, hat brim and pom pom white.

2 Paint a white line between his shoes to separate them. Paint a white highlight on the toe of each shoe. Paint his eyes blue; paint his cheeks, mouth and nose pink. Use white dimensional paint to squeeze the curl on his forehead and the hearts on his hat brim and cuffs. Squeeze a little paint into the hat pom pom and use the toothpick to pull out "fluffy" lines. Use the pen to fill in the eyes and go over all the pattern lines.

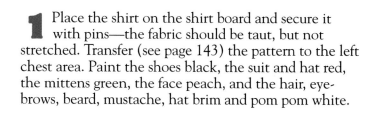

3 Brush a thin coat of clear glitter over the beard and mustache; let dry. Trace the pattern onto a piece of scrap paper and cut it out. Lay it over the painted Santa. Dip the toothbrush in green paint and use your thumb to spatter lightly around the Santa. Let dry and remove the protective paper.

Magnolia & Gold Box

by LeNae Gerig

9 ½" round papier-mâché box
1 ivory/gold silk pick with a 6" wide
   magnolia blossom, a 3" wide dogwood
   blossom, clusters of many ⅜"–½"
   gold/tan berries, and many 1½"–4"
   latex ivy and magnolia leaves
2½ yards of 2" wide ivory striped
   wire-edged ribbon
2½ yards of ¼" wide gold ribbon
1 oz. of white glittered dried baby's breath
spray paints: gold, ivory
gold spray webbing
low temperature glue gun and sticks or
   tacky craft glue

1 Spray the lid gold, inside and outside. Spray the box ivory, inside and outside; let dry. Spray the outside of the box with gold webbing; let dry.

2 Pull to separate the dogwood and magnolia stems. Cut the dogwood stem to 9" and the magnolia stem to 6". Glue them extending outward from the lid center with their ends overlapping. Arrange the leaves and berries to extend outward.

3 Hold the gold ribbon over the ivory ribbon and handle as one to make a puffy bow (see page 141) with a center loop, eight 3½" loops and 6" tails. Glue over the stem ends with the tails extending over the box edge.

4 Cut the baby's breath into 2"–4" sprigs. Glue the long sprigs among the leaves and flowers. Glue the short sprigs around the bow.

EMBELLISH IT!

Need a gift in a hurry? This is the section for you! We've included some smashing projects featuring great techniques. These projects are quick to do and involve decorating purchased pieces which look wonderful with just a bit of embellishment. Sometimes it's adding a little paint and a bow, as with the acrylic ornaments and the candles—or ribbons and a bit of floral filler, as with the stiffened crocheted forms. Very simple projects, wonderful results!

Sponging and spattering paints onto objects renders a terrific look with just a little effort and turns a plain piece into a special gift or ornament. Ribbon roses, lace, charms, braid and bows turn simple objects into beautiful and unique treasures with very little effort. Whether you're making them for your own decorating or for giving to special friends, this collection of projects will make your season cheerful and bright—very quickly!

FANCY FRAMES

by LeNae Gerig

for each frame:
30-gauge wire
low temperature glue gun and sticks
  or tacky craft glue

for the maple leaf frame:
6"x8" green/gold wooden frame
1 yard of 1½" wide gold mesh wire-
  edged ribbon
one 2¾" wide brass maple leaf charm

for the bow frame:
6½"x8½" gold wooden frame
4" round ivory crocheted doily
1 yard of ⅛" wide ivory satin ribbon
3¼" wide brass bow charm
black acrylic paint, matte acrylic sealer
#4 flat paintbrush, soft cloth

1 **Maple leaf frame:** (See the large photo above.) Use the ribbon to make a puffy bow (see page 141) with a center loop, six 2" loops and 3" tails. Trim each tail in an inverted V. Glue the bow to the top center of the frame, then glue the charm to the bow center.

2 **Bow frame:** Pinch the doily at the center and wire to secure it in a bow shape. Glue to the upper left corner of the frame. Use the ribbon to make a loopy bow (see page 140) with six 1½" loops, a 7" tail and a 9" tail. Glue the bow to the center of the doily. Loop and glue the 7" tail down the left side, the 9" tail over the top and down the right side as shown.

3 Paint the charm black. Immediately wipe with a soft cloth, removing paint from the high spots but leaving some in the grooves. Let dry; seal. Glue the charm to the bow center as shown in the large photo.

SPONGED POT

by LeNae Gerig

5 ½"x4 ⅜" terra cotta pot
matte acrylic sealer, 1" sponge paintbrush
acrylic paints: white, red, metallic gold
small natural sponge
paper plate, paper towels
2 yards of ⅟₁₆" wide red satin ribbon
2 yards of ⅟₁₆" wide gold cord

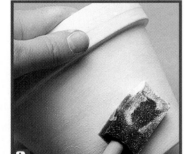

1 Use the sponge brush to apply sealer to the inside and outside of the pot; let dry.

2 Clean the brush and use it to apply two coats of white paint on the inside and outside of the pot; let dry.

3 Pour a quarter-sized puddle of red paint into a paper plate. Dampen the sponge, dip it into the paint and blot on paper towels. Sponge heavily around the sides of the pot and lightly onto the rim.

4 Rinse the sponge and repeat step 3 with gold paint, but sponge the gold lightly on the sides and heavily on the rim. Let dry and seal. Cut the ribbon and cord in half and hold all four lengths together. Tie around the pot below the rim as shown in the large photo, making a shoestring bow (see page 141) with 2" loops and 3"–4" tails.

SPONGED ORNAMENT

by LeNae Gerig

2 ½" wide red glass ball ornament
acrylic paints: gold, white
acrylic spray sealer
small natural sponge
paper plate, paper towels
6" of ⅛" wide gold cord
1 yard of 1 ¼" wide gold mesh ribbon
24-gauge wire
low temperature glue gun and sticks or tacky
    craft glue

(See the large photo.) Follow steps 3 and 4 at left to sponge the ball lightly with white, then with gold paint. Let dry; seal. Cut the ribbon in half and use each length to make a puffy bow (see page 141) with a center loop, four 1½" loops and no tails. Glue a bow to each side of the ball hanger. Insert the cord through the hanger, knot the ends and slide the knot down under the hanger.

DOUBLE HEART HANGINGS

by Kathy Thompson

for each decoration:
low temperature glue gun and
   sticks or tacky craft glue
for the wooden hearts:
two 3" wide wooden hearts
acrylic paints: white, burgundy
#6 flat paintbrush
24" of 1" wide white gathered
   lace
24" of ⅝" wide white satin
   picot ribbon
for the vine hearts:
two 3½" wide grapevine hearts
1 ⅔ yards of jute twine
two 1" wide burgundy dried
   rosebuds
¼ oz. of natural preserved
   baby's breath
¼ oz. of white preserved
   German statice
¼ oz. of green preserved
   plumosus

1 **Wooden hearts:** Paint both sides of each heart burgundy; let dry. Dip the brush handle into white paint and touch to the edge of a heart to make a dot. Repeat for each dot, making a scalloped border as shown.

2 Glue lace around the back of each heart, pinching to ease in fullness. Cut two 6" ribbon lengths and use each to make a shoestring bow (see page 141) with ¾" loops and ¾" tails. Glue one bow to each heart. Glue one end of the remaining ribbon to the top back of each heart for the hanger.

3 **Vine hearts:** Cut two 9" jute lengths and use each to make a shoestring bow (see page 141) with 1" loops and 1¾" tails. Glue one bow to each heart. Cut an 18" and a 24" jute length. Glue one end of each length to the top back of each heart. Hold the centers together, adjusting so the hearts hang at different heights, and knot 1" below the top for the hanger.

4 Glue a rosebud to the bottom of each heart. Cut the statice into 1"–1½" sprigs; glue half around each rosebud. Cut the baby's breath into 1½" sprigs and the plumosus to 2" sprigs. Glue around the rosebuds as shown.

"MARBLE" ORNAMENTS by LeNae Gerig

for each ornament:
12" length of monofila-
    ment nylon fishing line
needle
30-gauge wire
tacky craft glue
low temperature glue gun
    and sticks (optional)

for the ball ornament:
3" wide clear acrylic ball
acrylic paints: gold, purple
2 yards of 1½" wide gold
    mesh wire-edged ribbon

for the heart ornament:
4" wide clear iridescent
    acrylic heart ornament
acrylic paints: silver, red,
    dark green
2 yards of 1½" wide silver
    mesh wire-edged ribbon

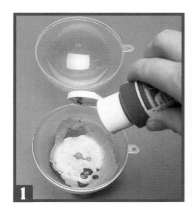

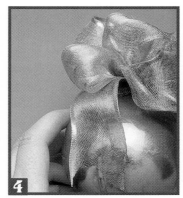

1 **Ball ornament:** Separate the halves and pour about two tablespoons each of gold and purple paint into one half.

2 Run a bead of tacky glue around the rim of one half, then rejoin the halves. Gently tip the ornament back and forth so the paint runs across the inside surface.

3 Briskly shake the ornament to marble the paint and cover the entire inner surface. Let dry undisturbed for 24 hours.

4 Use the gold ribbon to make a puffy bow (see page 141) with a center loop, ten 2" loops and 4" tails. Trim each tail in an inverted V. Glue the bow to the top of the ornament; loop and glue the tails down the side seams. Thread the nylon line on the needle and take a stitch through the center loop, then knot the ends together for a hanger.

5 **Heart ornament:** Follow steps 1–3, using the silver, red and dark green paints. Follow step 4 to make a puffy bow from the silver ribbon.

GOLD & GREEN CANDLESTICKS

by LeNae Gerig

two 7" tall turned wood
candlesticks
two 12" long dark green taper can-
dles
2⅔ yards of 1½" wide dark green
taffeta ribbon with gold wired
edges
acrylic paints: dark green, metallic
gold
gold spray paint
gold spray glitter
matte acrylic spray sealer
old toothbrush, newspapers
24-gauge wire
low temperature glue gun and sticks
or tacky craft glue

1 Spread out the newspapers to protect the work surface. Spray the candles with sealer; let dry. Dip the toothbrush into gold acrylic paint and use your thumb to spatter the candles as shown; let dry.

2 Spray the candlesticks gold; let dry. Clean the toothbrush and use it to spatter the candlesticks with green paint; let dry.

3 Cut the ribbon in half and use each half to make an oblong bow (see page 140) with a center loop, two 1½" loops, four 2" loops and 4" tails. Spray the bows with glitter. Glue one at an angle to the top of each candlestick as shown in the large photo. Insert the candles into the candlesticks.

SPATTERED PILLAR CANDLE

by LeNae Gerig

2¾"x8¾" burgundy pillar
candle
1⅛ yards of 1½" wide gold
mesh wire-edged ribbon
with burgundy and blue
flecks
matte acrylic spray sealer
gold acrylic paint
old toothbrush, newspapers
24-gauge wire
low temperature glue gun and
sticks or tacky craft glue

Spray the candle with sealer; let dry. Follow step 1 above to spatter it gold. Use the ribbon to make a puffy bow (see page 141) with a center loop, six 2" loops and one 10" tail. 6" below the candle top, wrap the tail around the candle and glue the bow at an angle to the tail.

BEAUTIFIED BOXES by LeNae Gerig

for each box:
3" round ivory Adornables™ plastic box
low temperature glue gun and sticks or tacky craft glue

for the cherub box:
2" wide brass cherub charm
matte acrylic spray sealer
acrylic paints: ivory, metallic gold
#6 flat paintbrush, soft cloth
small natural sponge, paper plate, paper towels

for the floral box:
12" of ½" wide mauve gimp braid
three ½" wide mauve ribbon roses
twelve 1" long sprigs of green preserved plumosus
five 1" long sprigs of white dried German statice

side view

1 **Cherub box:** Paint the charm ivory. Immediately wipe with a soft cloth, removing paint from the high spots but leaving some in the grooves. Let dry. Spray the charm and the box with sealer.

2 Pour a 2" puddle of gold paint in a paper plate. Dampen the sponge, dip it into the paint and blot on paper towels. Sponge the box, letting some ivory show through. Let dry and spray again with sealer. Glue the charm to the lid.

3 **Floral box:** Glue braid around the lower edge of the box lid, letting it extend a scant ⅛" below the edge. Glue the roses in a triangle to the center top. Glue the statice and fern extending outward around the roses.

LACY HEART

by Rona Riley

one 4" wide clear acrylic heart
¼ yard of ¾" wide white
   gathered lace
5" square of white flat lace
   fabric
1 ½ yards of ⅛" wide white
   satin ribbon
seven 6mm clear round
   acrylic beads
one 1" wide white ribbon rose
one ⅝" wide white ribbon rose
ultra-fine iridescent glitter
#8 flat paintbrush
clothespins
flexible wire beading needle
bamboo skewer
tacky craft glue

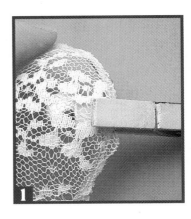

1 Separate the heart halves and brush glue on the rim of the front half. Place the lace fabric over the heart and pull taut over the rim. Secure with clothespins until dry; trim excess fabric.

2 Glue gathered lace around the rim. Rejoin the halves.

3 Tie 12" of ribbon through the tab for a hanger. Cut the remaining ribbon into 3½"–8" lengths and knot each 1" from one end. Use the needle to thread a bead onto each ribbon and slide it down to the knot. Hold all the ribbons together at the unknotted ends and glue to the bottom back of the heart.

4 Wrap the rose stems around a skewer to curl them. Glue to the heart top. Brush the small rose lightly with glue, then sprinkle with glitter.

FOUR ORNAMENTS by Sue Kahr

(listed clockwise from the center top of the photo)

for the dove:
one 4½" wide clear acrylic dove
   with outstretched wings and a gold cord hanger
18" of ³/₁₆" wide ecru satin picot ribbon
18" of ¼" wide white satin ribbon
12" of 3mm ivory iridescent fused pearls
one 1" wide white ribbon rose

for the cello:
one 4" long capiz shell cello
   with a gold cord hanger
12" of ³/₁₆" wide ecru satin picot ribbon
12" of ⅜" wide ivory flat lace ribbon
one ⅜" wide white ribbon rose

for the bell:
one 2" wide gold jingle bell
   with a gold cord hanger
9" of 1⅛" wide ivory gathered lace
needle, white thread
18" of ½" wide ecru satin picot ribbon
18" of ¼" wide white satin ribbon
12" of 3mm ivory iridescent fused pearls
one 1" wide white ribbon rose

for the cherub:
one 3" long clear acrylic cherub
   with gold wings and a gold cord hanger
18" of ³/₁₆" wide ecru satin picot ribbon
18" of ¼" wide white satin ribbon
12" of 3mm ivory iridescent fused pearls
one ⅜" wide white ribbon rose

for each ornament:
low temperature glue gun and sticks or tacky craft glue

1 Dove: Glue the center of the pearl length to the dove's back between the wings. Hold the ribbons together and make a shoestring bow (see page 141) with 1¼" loops and 6½"–7" tails. Glue over the pearls as shown; glue the rose into the bow center.

2 Cello: Use the lace to make a shoestring bow with ¾" loops and 3½" tails; glue at an angle to the right shoulder of the cello. Use the ribbon to make a shoestring bow with ½" loops and 3½" tails. Glue it to the lace bow center. Twirl and glue the tails as shown in the large photo. Glue the rose into the bow center.

3 Bell: Sew a running stitch along the bound edge of the lace and gather it tightly around the bell top; glue to secure. Glue the center of the pearl length in front of the hanger. Hold the ribbons together and make a shoestring bow with 1" loops and 6"–6½"" tails. Glue over the pearls as shown; glue the rose into the bow center.

4 Cherub: Follow step 1, but make the bow with 1" loops.

back view

BABY BIRDHOUSES

by LeNae Gerig

wooden mini birdhouses: one 3"x2½",
  one 2¼"x2½"
18" of ⅝" wide red satin ribbon
18" of ⅝" wide green satin ribbon
acrylic paints: white, red, dark green
#6 flat paintbrush
round wooden toothpicks
fine sandpaper, soft cloth
low temperature glue gun and sticks or
  tacky craft glue

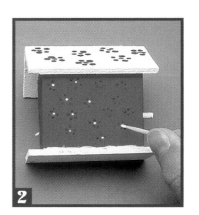

1 Lightly sand the birdhouses to remove any rough edges. **White/red birdhouse:** Paint the sides of the 2¼"x2½" house red. Paint the roof, base, perch and inside the door-hole white. Let dry.

2 For each roof flower: Dip the paintbrush handle in green paint and touch to the roof to make a dot. Repeat for a circle of five green dots, then make a red dot in the center. Make seven flowers evenly spaced on each side of the roof. Make green dots around the hole. Use a toothpick to dot green flowers and white centers evenly spaced around the front, back and sides of the house.

3 **Red/green birdhouse:** Paint the 3" wide house green with a red roof, base, perch and hole. Let dry. Follow step 2 to decorate with dot flowers, but make white flowers with green centers on the roof and white flowers with red centers on the sides. Make white dots around the hole.

4 **Bows:** Cut a 1½" red ribbon length and set aside. Use the remaining red ribbon to make a loopy bow (see page 140) with a 5" center loop (for the hanger), two 1" loops and no tails. Wrap the center with the 1½" length, gluing to secure. Glue the bow to the top of the white/red house. Repeat to make a green bow and glue it to the top of the red/green house.

GOLD BALL ORNAMENT

by LeNae Gerig

one 3" wide Styrofoam® ball
2 yards of 1" wide ivory satin ribbon
gold acrylic paint, #10 flat paintbrush
20" of ½" wide ivory gimp braid
1 yard of 6mm ivory fused pearls
16" of ivory/gold rose braid
1 yard of 1/16" wide gold cord
one 5/8" wide pearl shank button
one 3" long ivory satin tassel
low temperature glue gun and sticks or tacky craft glue

top view

top view

1 Paint the ball gold; let dry. Glue the gimp as shown, dividing the ball into quarters.

2 Cut the pearls into eight 4½" lengths and glue one on each side of each section of gimp.

top view

3 Glue 4" lengths of rose braid between the gimp sections. Glue the tassel to the bottom.

4 Use the ribbon to make a puffy bow (see page 141) with twelve 2" loops and no tails. Glue to the center top. Use the cord to make a loopy bow (see page 140) with a 3½" center loop (for the hanger), eight 1½" loops and no tails. Glue to the center of the first bow. Glue the button into the hanger loop.

LENAE'S CROCHETS

by
LeNae
Gerig

STAR & ROSES

one 4" wide ivory stiffened crocheted doily star
18" of ¼" wide dark green satin ribbon
two ½" wide ivory ribbon roses
two ⅜" wide burgundy rosebuds
eight 1" long sprigs of white dried baby's breath
one ½" wide brass heart charm
24-gauge wire
6" of metallic gold thread
low temperature glue gun and sticks or tacky craft glue

1 Use the ribbon to make a puffy bow (see page 141) with ten 1" loops. Glue to the star center. Glue the roses to the bow center, alternating colors.

2 Glue baby's breath around and among the roses. Glue the charm extending to the lower right. For a hanger, knot the thread through a loop in the top point of the star.

POTPOURRI HAT

one 5" round ivory stiffened crocheted doily hat
one 1¼" wide stiffened crocheted flower doily
24" of ¼" wide mauve satin ribbon
one ½" wide mauve ribbon rose
eight 1½" long sprigs of white dried baby's breath
3½" square of ivory tulle net fabric
⅛ cup of potpourri
6" of metallic gold thread
low temperature glue gun and sticks or tacky craft glue

1 Turn the hat upside down and fill the crown with potpourri. Run a bead of glue around the rim, press the tulle into it and let set. Trim excess tulle.

2 Turn the hat right side up and glue ribbon around the crown. Use the remaining ribbon to make a shoe-string bow (see page 141) with 1" loops and 3½" tails. Glue over the ends of the ribbon hatband; knot the tails. Glue the flower doily into the bow center and the rose into the doily center. Glue baby's breath around the doily. For a hanger, knot the thread through a loop of the hat opposite the bow.

SEE-THROUGH BALL

one 2½" round stiffened crocheted doily ball with a
    gold thread hanger
6" of 1" wide ivory gathered lace
12" of ⅛" wide mauve satin ribbon
ribbon roses: three ½" wide ivory, three ½" wide
    mauve, three ⅜" wide burgundy buds
six 1" sprigs of white dried baby's breath
six 1½"–2" sprigs of green preserved plumosus
needle, ivory thread
low temperature glue gun and sticks or tacky craft
    glue

1 Sew a run-
ning stitch
along the bound
edge of the lace
and gather tightly
around the hang-
er; glue to secure.
Use the ribbon to
make a loopy
bow (see page
140) with four

1½" loops and no tails. Glue to the lace center.
Glue two of each color rose to the bow center
as shown. Glue the remaining roses in a triangle to the bottom of the ball as shown in the
large photo.

2 Glue baby's breath among the roses and
bow loops. Repeat with the plumosus.

BERIBBONED HEART

one 3¾" wide white stiffened crocheted doily heart
27" of 3/16" wide metallic gold ribbon
ribbon roses: two ½" wide ivory, two ½" wide mauve, two ⅜" wide burgundy buds
one 3" long mauve tassel
low temperature glue gun and sticks or tacky craft glue

1 Cut a 6" ribbon length for the hanger. Thread one end front to back through a loop
at the top of one heart shoulder; repeat for the other end. Knot each end at the back
to prevent it slipping out of the loop. Insert the loop of the tassel through the heart
point and glue in back.

2 Use the remaining ribbon to make a loopy bow (see page 140) with four 1" loops, a
7" tail and a 10" tail. Glue the bow to the left shoulder of the heart. Loop and glue
the short tail down the left side; repeat with the long tail around the right side, ending
1" above the point.

3 Glue three roses to the bow center and three over the glued area of the tails as
shown in the large photo.

Frosty Friendlies

Let it snow! Let it snow! Let it snow! These charming fellows don't mind if you bring them inside to decorate your tree, either—they won't melt! In fact, they'll hang around to provide joy throughout many holiday seasons to come.

Jolly snowmen are being seen in all the fine, trendy gift shops and have become very popular as Christmas decorations. They provide charm, whimsy and memories of Christmases past, bringing warmth and cheer to the holidays.

And these snowmen aren't just for the Christmas tree! There is a smiling snowman canister that is just begging to hold special recipes for fudge or holiday cookies as a unique gift for a loved one. You can tie many of these snowmen onto packages for a great finish to the wrappings. Or attach them to wreaths, centerpieces and swags, developing a theme and carrying it throughout the house. We've also included a sweet snowman pin to be worn on the lapel of a special jacket or vest. And these guys would make a great collection to display on a prominent shelf or mantel.

Snowmen are popular fellows, carrying the cheer of the holiday through the New Year celebrations and becoming not just Christmas decorations, but winter embellishments for your home. We hope you enjoy creating these special fellows and that they add a festive air to your celebrations!

103

Freddy Snowman

by Marilyn Holbrook

polymer clay (see page 143):
  white, green, burgundy, black,
  orange
2" long broom
textured snow paint (such as Snow
  Tex™ or Snow Accents™)
craft stick or flat paintbrush
round wooden toothpicks
sharp knife
black acrylic paint
pink powdered blush, cotton swab
2" long gold eye pin

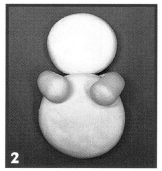

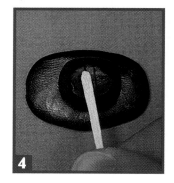

actual height 3½"

head (cut away
shaded area)

arm

body

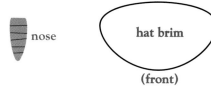
nose

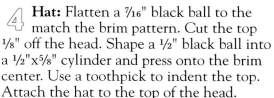
hat brim

(front)

scarf

1 Body: Flatten a ¾" white ball to match the body pattern. Flatten a ⅝" white ball to match the head pattern. Insert half a toothpick into the top of the body. Push the head onto the exposed toothpick.

2 Arms: Shape two ½" white balls to match the arm pattern. Attach the pointed end of each to the neck back, bending the rounded end to the front. Smooth the shoulder ends into the body.

3 Scarf: Roll a ⁵⁄₁₆" green ball and one of burgundy. Shape each into a 3" long log and twist together, then flatten to a 6"x⅜" rectangle. Use a knife to cut fringe in each end. Wrap it around the neck and press it down between the arms, overlapping one end as shown. Insert the broom between the body and left arm to make a hole, then remove it.

4 Hat: Flatten a ⁷⁄₁₆" black ball to the match the brim pattern. Cut the top ⅛" off the head. Shape a ½" black ball into a ½"x⅝" cylinder and press onto the brim center. Use a toothpick to indent the top. Attach the hat to the top of the head.

5 Nose: Shape a ¼" orange ball into a cone and use the knife to texture it. Trim the wide end to make a flat surface. Press onto the face and use a toothpick to smooth the edges. Insert an eye pin into the top of the hat. Bake at 250° for 30 minutes (or according to the clay manufacturer's instructions). Let cool. Dip a toothpick into black paint and dot two eyes. Make a row of dots for the mouth. Blush the cheeks. Brush a few strokes of snow paint over the snowman for a rougher texture. Replace the broom through the hole in the left arm.

Dancing Snowman Gift Box

by LeNae Gerig

8½" square papier-mâché box
2¼ yards of ¾" wide red/green/gold plaid ribbon
spray paints: dark green, white
two 1½" long branched twigs
½" buttons: 1 red, 1 green
textured snow paint (such as Snow Tex™ or Snow
   Accents™)
black dimensional paint
acrylic paints: white, orange
paintbrushes: #4 flat, #0/10 liner
tracing paper, transfer paper, pencil
low temperature glue gun and sticks or
   tacky craft glue

1 Spray the inside and outside of the box green; let dry.
Trace the patterns. Center the circle pattern on the
lid and lightly spray white paint over the top—some will
blur the circle edge as shown. Remove the pattern and
lightly mist the box sides and lid rim with white; let dry.

2 Lay the body pattern in the center of the circle and
trace only the gray outline. Use the flat brush to
paint the snowman white; let dry. Brush on textured paint
to fill the snowman; let dry.

**¼ circle pattern: fold tracing paper in
fourths and place straight edges on folds.**

3 Transfer (see page 143) the rest of the pattern.
Squeeze black dimensional paint for the hat, boots,
eyes and mouth. Use the liner brush to paint black eyebrows and an orange nose. Add snow texture to the boot
bottoms. Glue the twigs and buttons as shown by the gray
dashed lines.

4 Glue ribbon to the top edge of the lid, mitering the
corners as shown; trim excess. Glue ribbon around
the center of the box sides, overlapping the ends; trim
excess. Cut a 2" and a 7" ribbon length. Make a loop with
the 7" length and wrap the 2" length around the center to
form a bow. Glue to the center front ribbon as shown in
the large photo.

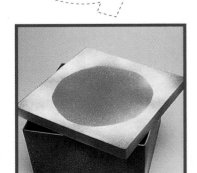

1

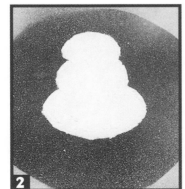

2

3

4

by Joann Pearson

one 1" wide wood ball
one ½" white pom pom
3" square of red ribbing fabric
1"x7" piece of red/green plaid fabric
red thread
acrylic paints: black, white, orange
#6 flat paintbrush
pink powdered blush, cotton swab
¾" long pin back
low temperature glue gun and sticks
    or tacky craft glue

actual height 5" including scarf

1 **Hat:** Glue opposite edges of the ribbing together, forming a tube with the ribs running lengthwise. Wrap thread tightly around one end and knot to secure. Turn seam side in. Fold the lower edge up ¼", then ⅜" to form a brim.

2 Paint the ball white; let dry. Glue the hat onto the ball, pulling it down in back. Glue the pom pom to the hat tip.

3 **Scarf:** Fray the edges of the plaid fabric. Fold in half lengthwise and knot loosely around your finger. Slide the knot off and glue the loop to the bottom of the ball with the knot at one side.

4 Refer to the face pattern to paint an orange nose in the center of the face. Dip the handle of the paintbrush in black and touch to the face to dot the eyes; repeat for the mouth dots. Blush the cheeks. Glue the pin to the back of the head.

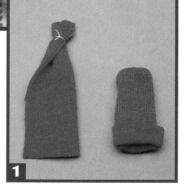

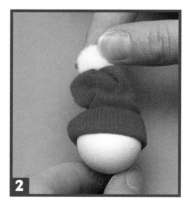

Twisty the Snowman

by Nancy Overmyer

4" wide twisted paper ribbon:
25" of white, 8" of brown
one 1½" wide Styrofoam® ball
one ⅜" wide brown pom pom
12" of ⅞" wide red/green plaid ribbon
1"x5" piece of lightweight cardboard
3"x5" piece of of black felt
black acrylic paint
#00 liner paintbrush
round wooden toothpick
20-gauge wire, wire cutters
low temperature glue gun and sticks or
    tacky craft glue

2" circle

actual height 9"

1 **Head:** Untwist the white paper ribbon; cut a 10" length. Place the foam ball 2" from one end and wrap the ribbon around it; glue the edges together. Twist both ends tightly close to the ball; wire to secure.

2 **Body:** Fold the remaining white paper ribbon in half crosswise. Gather ½" from the ends, forming a ruffle, and insert the stem of the head down through the ruffle. Push the ruffle close to the head and wire tightly just below it.

3 **Face:** Transfer (see page 143) the face pattern. Paint the eyes and mouth black. Glue the pom pom for his nose. **Hat:** From the black felt, cut two 2" circles and a 1"x5" strip. Glue the cardboard ends together to form a 1¼" wide tube. Glue a felt circle over one open end of the tube, folding it down over the sides. Glue the strip around the tube, then glue

the remaining circle to the other end. Cut the paper ribbon on the top of the head close to the wire; glue the hat onto his head.

4 **Arms:** Untwist 1" on each end of the brown paper ribbon and cut into three fingers. Twist each finger. Glue the arms between the body layers. **Scarf:** Cut fringe in the ends of the plaid ribbon. Wrap it around his neck, knot, and glue to secure.

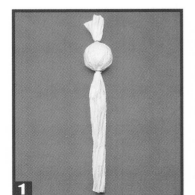

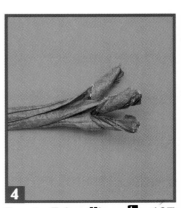

Goody Jar

by Marilyn Gossett

one 3⅜"x8" clear glass apothecary jar with a 2" ball on the lid
1½"x16" strip of green/beige plaid fabric
4"x8" piece of burgundy/black checked fabric
½" wide heart buttons: 2 burgundy, 2 green
9" of jute twine
acrylic paints: white, peach, orange, black
#4 round paintbrush
waxed paper, paper towels
low temperature glue gun and sticks or tacky craft glue

Note: Wash the jar bottom in warm, not hot, water; wipe the lid with a damp cloth only.

1 **Head:** Remove the lid from the jar, turn over and pour in white paint. Tip and tilt the lid until the paint completely coats the inner surface. Pour excess back into the paint container. Set the lid on waxed paper to dry overnight.

2 **Face:** Refer to the pattern. Just above the widest part of the ball, paint two ½" peach circles ⅝" apart. Let dry. Dip the paintbrush handle in white paint and dot the cheek highlights. Wipe the brush handle clean, dip in black paint and dot the eyes and mouth. Paint the nose orange.

3 Glue one button in the center front of the flared area of the lid. Glue the remaining buttons ⅝" apart down the jar front, alternating colors. **Scarf:** Fray the edges of the green fabric and knot it around his neck.

4 **Hat:** Fray the edges of the checked fabric. Fold up ½" along one long edge. Wrap the hat around his head with the folded edge at the bottom. Glue in place, overlapping and gluing the short edges together at the back. Gather the hat top 1" below the top and tie with the jute, making a shoestring bow (see page 141) with 1" loops and 1½" tails.

Mr. Snowball

by Suzanne Jones

Styrofoam® balls: one 2", one 2½"
2" of ⅛" wooden dowel
pencil sharpener
wire cutters
2" wide black felt hat
two 2" long forked twigs
⅜" wide buttons: 1 red, 1 green
black half-round beads: two 6mm, four 3mm
¾"x9" strip of green/cream checked fabric
orange acrylic paint, paintbrush
round wooden toothpick
needle, 9" of gold thread
tacky craft glue

actual height 4½"

1. **Body:** Roll the foam balls on a firm surface, compressing them to look like packed snow. Be careful to keep them round. Barely flatten one side of each ball. Insert a toothpick halfway into the center of the flat area of the larger ball. Remove, apply glue and reinsert. Press the other ball onto the toothpick so its flat area matches that of the other ball. Remove, apply glue to the toothpick and replace the ball. Let the glue set.

2. **Hat:** Thread the gold thread onto the needle. Poke the needle through the hat top, inside to out, then back to the inside ⅛" away. Remove the needle and knot the thread ends inside the hat. Glue the hat to the head. Curve the brim front upward.

3. **Nose:** Use the pencil sharpener to sharpen the dowel. Paint the sharpened end orange; let dry. Cut to 1" long and glue into the center front of the face. Glue the 6mm beads above it for eyes and the 3mm beads for the mouth.

4. Fray the edges of the fabric strip and knot around his neck for a scarf. Glue the buttons to his tummy. Insert the twigs into his sides as shown. Remove, apply glue and reinsert.

actual height 2¾"

Stuffed Snowman

by Marilyn Gossett

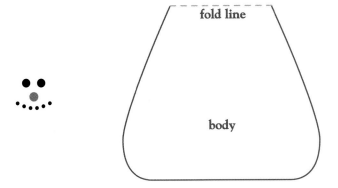

fold line

body

one ¾" round wooden bead
3"x4" piece of white broadcloth fabric
6" of ⅜" wide green/red plaid ribbon
1⅛"x¾" black plastic top hat
one ½" wide white button
1"x1⅜" wooden Christmas tree cutout
acrylic paints: green, red, white, orange, black
small paintbrush
round wooden toothpick
8" of gold thread
tracing paper, pencil
sewing machine or needle and white thread
candle and matches or lighter
polyester fiberfill
low temperature glue gun and sticks or tacky craft glue

1 **Body:** Tear a ½" strip from one 4" edge of the fabric. Knot the center of the strip and set aside. Trace the body pattern and cut two body pieces from the remaining fabric. Sew the body pieces together in a ¼" seam, leaving the top open. Clip curves and turn right side out. Stuff tightly and sew the opening closed. To form the arms, place the knot of the 4" strip at the center front and glue the ends to the top back.

2 **Head:** Paint the bead white; let dry. Referring to the pattern, dip the handle of the paintbrush in orange paint and touch to the center front to dot the nose. Dot the eyes with black. Dip the toothpick in black paint to dot the mouth. Let dry, then glue to the body.

3 **Scarf:** Trim the ribbon ends diagonally. Knot the ribbon around his neck with the knot slightly left of the center front. **Tree:** Paint the wooden cutout green. Dip the handle of the paintbrush in red paint to dot the ornaments; let dry. Glue the tree to his hands.

4 **Hat:** Heat the tip of the needle in a flame and make a hole through the center top of the hat. Insert both ends of the gold thread through the hole, outside to inside, and knot them together. Pull the knot up inside the hat and glue to secure. Glue the hat to his head.

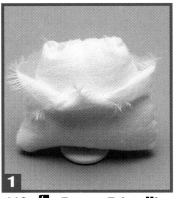

1

3

2

4

Peg Snowman

by Jackie Zars

2¼" tall wooden doll peg
polymer clay (see page 143): black, white
acrylic paints: white, black, peach, orange
paintbrushes: #0 round, ¼" flat
6" of ⅜" wide red/green plaid ribbon
round wooden toothpick
drill with 5/32" or 1/16" bit
3" of 30-gauge wire, pliers
8" of nylon monofilament fishing line
low temperature glue gun and sticks or tacky craft glue

arms

hat brim   hat crown

1 Paint the peg white; let dry. Referring to the face pattern, dip the paintbrush handle into black paint to dot the eyes. Dip the toothpick into black to dot the mouth.

2 Drill a ⅛" deep hole at the nose point. Paint ⅜" on one end of the toothpick orange; let dry. Cut off the painted area and glue into the hole. Blend peach paint with an equal amount of water and paint the cheeks.

3 **Arms:** Roll a 3½"x⅜" log of white clay. Attach the center to the back of the neck and wrap the arms to the front as shown (notice one is lower than the other). Push the broom handle through his right hand to make a hole; remove.

4 **Hat:** Flatten a ⅝" black clay ball to a 1⅛" wide circle. Place a dab of tacky glue on the top of his head and press the circle onto it. Shape a ¾" black ball into a cylinder and press onto the center of the circle. Push down on the top with your finger to flatten it slightly. Wrap the wire around the paintbrush handle and twist the ends together, then insert the twisted ends into the top of the hat to make a hanger. Bake him at 250° for 30 minutes (or according to the clay manufacturer's instructions); let cool. Glue the ribbon around his neck for a scarf, knotting it at his left side. Glue the broom into his hand. Insert the nylon line through the hanger and knot the ends.

actual height 3"

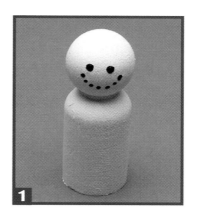

1

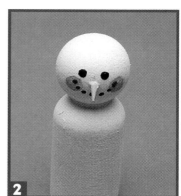

2

3

4

Model Magic® Snowman

by Joann Pearson

actual height 3½"

4-oz. package of Model Magic®
    air-dry clay
2" wide black felt hat
8" long red/green knitted scarf
two 2½" long forked twigs
waxed paper
acrylic paints: black, orange
½" flat paintbrush
low temperature glue gun and
    sticks or tacky craft glue

1. Work on waxed paper. Shape a 1¾" clay ball; flatten the bottom slightly. Shape a 1½" ball and press onto the top of the first ball.

2. Shape a ¾" long cone and press in place for a nose. Insert the twigs for arms. Dry for 24 hours.

3. Dip the paintbrush handle in black paint and touch to dot the eyes; repeat for the mouth and buttons. Paint the nose orange.

4. Tie the scarf around his neck, knotting it at one side. Glue the hat onto his head, turning the brim front down as shown.

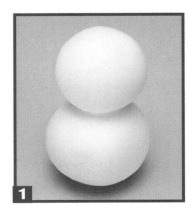

Mini Snow Boy

by Susan Capper

one 2" tall wooden doll peg
1⅛"x⅝" black plastic hat
6" of ¼" wide red satin ribbon
acrylic paint: white, red, black
#4 flat paintbrush
black fine-tip permanent pen
needle, 9" of gold thread
candle and matches or lighter
polymer clay (see page 143): orange, yellow
round wooden toothpick, wire cutters
low temperature glue gun and sticks or tacky craft glue

1 Paint the peg white; let dry and recoat if needed. Refer to the face pattern. Dip the paintbrush handle in red paint and dot the cheeks.

2 Dip the paintbrush handle in black to dot the eyes and buttons. Draw the mouth with the pen.

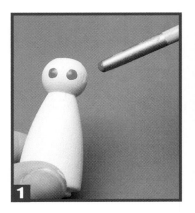

3 Roll a ⅜" long cone of orange clay. Attach to the head, using a bit of tacky glue for extra security. Flatten a ½" yellow ball to match the broom pattern. Attach to the body with a dab of glue. Use the toothpick to imprint straw lines, then cut the toothpick to 1½" long and insert the point into the broom top. Bake at 225° for 30–45 minutes (or according to the clay manufacturer's instructions).

4 Wrap the ribbon around his neck for a scarf, knotting it at one side. **Hat:** Heat the needle point in a flame and make a hole through the center top. Insert both ends of the gold thread through the hole, outside to inside, and knot them together. Pull the knot up inside the hat and glue to secure. Glue the hat to his head.

actual height 2½"

broom

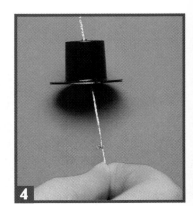

TREE TREASURES

Christmas ornaments make the tree! Or the wreath, or the centerpiece, or even the window. We've gathered a diverse collection of quick and easy ornaments for you to make for yourself or to give as gifts. They include lots of adorable animals, special teacher ornaments, whimsical elves, delightful bunnies, Victorian ornaments—even clever cut-outs made from cinnamon and applesauce!

Ornaments can be used in so many different ways. Adding several coordinating ornaments among the sprigs of an evergreen wreath displayed on a door helps welcome the season. Tucking a couple of Victorian ornaments into a candle centerpiece adds elegance. Tying pine cone elves to a garland, then draping it across a mantle or windowsill, brings charm and whimsy into the home.

A great finish to a special gift is a unique ornament tied to the bow center—the wrapping then becomes part of the gift, individualizing it. A strong button magnet can be glued to the back of an ornament, allowing it to be kept on the refrigerator, dutifully holding important messages all year round. This works especially well on flat ornaments such as those made from dough or fabric.

Or choose several ornaments which fit into one category, such as animals, Victorian, country, woodland, etc., and make many of each from coordinating materials, then decorate the entire tree in that theme. Although this could become quite an ambitious project, adding in similarly-themed, ready-made decorations among the handmade versions can stretch the pieces enough to decorate more than just a tree. Maybe a room…or even a whole house?

However you choose to use or display the ornaments, we've put together a great collection of clever, cute and pretty pieces for you to create to match your own decor.

Kittens in Mittens

by Suzanne Jones

6" square of white felt
needle and white thread
24" of pink yarn
18" of nylon monofilament fishing line
four 3mm half-round black beads
polyester fiberfill
gray pom poms: two 1½", ten ¼"
four ¼" white pom poms
two 5mm pink pom poms
tracing paper, pencil
low temperature glue gun and sticks or tacky craft glue

actual height 4½"

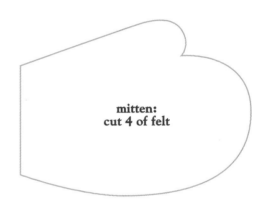

mitten:
cut 4 of felt

1 Mittens: Fold the felt in half. Trace the mitten pattern twice onto the top layer and cut out. Glue together around the curved edges, leaving the tops open.

2 Run a wide bead of glue around the top of one mitten. Begin at the back seam and wrap yarn three times around the top. Glue the other end of the yarn around the other mitten in the same way—there will be about 10" of yarn between them.

3 For each kitten: Glue a 1½" pom pom into a mitten opening. Trim two ¼" gray pom poms into triangles and glue for the ears. Glue two ¼" gray pom poms to the mitten top as shown for paws.

4 Glue two ¼" white pom poms for the muzzle, a pink pom pom for the nose and two beads for eyes. Glue three ¾" nylon line lengths for whiskers. Trim the whisker ends. Hold the ornament by the yarn and adjust the mittens to hang at different heights. Glue the mittens together at the seams as shown in the large photo.

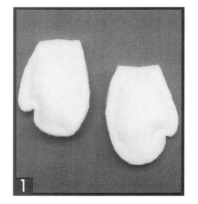

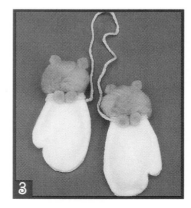

Opossums

by Suzanne Jones

one 4" long artificial candy cane
gray pom poms: two 1", four ¾", two ½", four ¼"
three 5mm peach pom poms
two 4mm black half-round beads
4 black seed beads
9" of ⅛" wide dark green satin ribbon
18" of red embroidery floss
12" of white cloth-covered 30-gauge wire
9" of nylon monofilament fishing line
low temperature glue gun and sticks or tacky craft glue

actual width 4½"

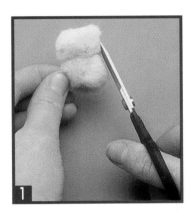

1 **Mama:** Glue the 1" pom poms together. Trim the top pom pom (the head) to form a pointed snout.

2 Glue ½" pom poms for ears, a peach pom pom for the nose and the 4mm beads for eyes. Wrap the floss around her neck and tie in a shoestring bow (see page 141) with ½" loops and ½" tails. Trim excess floss and set aside for step 4. **Tail:** Cut two 3" lengths of wire and twist together. Dip one end in glue and insert into the bottom of the body.

3 Make two babies. **For each baby:** Glue two ½" pom poms together, trim and glue on a nose as for Mama. Use two seed beads for eyes and ¼" pom poms for ears.

4 Tie embroidery floss around the neck in a shoestring bow with ¼" loops and ¼" tails. Use a 2½" single wire length for the tail. Wrap the tails of all three opossums around the candy cane as shown in the large photo. Tie one end of the nylon line around each end of the straight section of the candy cane; secure with glue. Use the ribbon to make a shoestring bow with ½" loops and ½" tails. Glue to the curved end of the cane.

Little Dough Santa

by Nancy Overmyer

dough (see page 142): white, red, peach
two 4mm black beads
polymer sealer (such as Envirotex Lite® or UltraGlo®)
white acrylic paint, #00 liner paintbrush
X-acto® knife, foil-lined cookie sheet
pink powdered blush, cotton swab
1½" of 30-gauge wire
6" of gold cord
low temperature glue gun and sticks or tacky craft glue

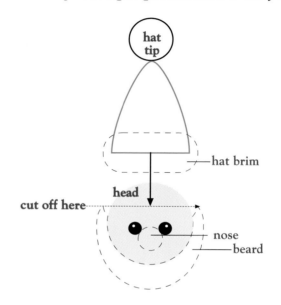

actual height 2½"

For a charming holiday pin, omit the hanger and glue on a ¾" pin back.

1 Roll a ¾" ball of peach dough and flatten slightly. Cut off the top ¼ and set aside for step 2 . Shape a ¾" red ball into a cone, flatten and press the bottom to the cut edge of the peach ball.

2 Roll a ¼"x2½" white rope and attach for a hat brim. Roll a ⅜" white ball for the hat tip. Roll a ⅜"x2¾" white rope and curve it around the bottom of his face for the beard. Flatten, then texture it with a knife.

3 Roll a ¼" peach ball and attach for the nose. For eyes, press a bead into the dough on each side of the nose. Press the knife tip into the bottom left face to imprint a mouth. Curve the wire around a pencil to form a hanging loop; twist the ends together and insert into the top back of the hat. Bake at 325° until hard. Blush his cheeks. Paint a white highlight in each eye. Seal; let dry. Insert the gold cord through the hanger and knot the ends together.

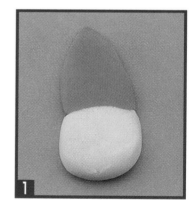

Puppy on a Pillow

by Joan Zeigler

two 3½" squares of red/white heart print fabric
polyester fiberfill
needle and red thread, sewing machine (optional)
felt: 3" square of black, 1" square of pink
9" length of ⅛" wide dark green satin ribbon
two 3mm black beads
6" of nylon monofilament fishing line
tan pom poms: one 1½", one 1", one ¾", four ½"
one 5mm black pom pom
low temperature glue gun and sticks or tacky craft glue

actual size 3" square

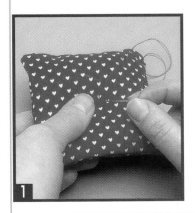

3½" square

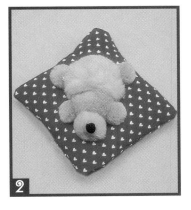

1 **Pillow:** Place the fabric right sides together and sew with a ¼" seam, leaving a 1½" opening on one side. Clip the corners diagonally and turn right side out. Stuff lightly and hand sew the opening closed. Take a small stitch through the center of the pillow, pull the thread up tightly and knot.

2 **Puppy:** Glue the 1½", 1" and ¾" pom poms together in a row, forming a body, head and muzzle. Glue the ½" pom poms for feet and the black pom pom for a nose. Glue the puppy to the pillow center.

3 Trace the patterns. Cut two ears and one tail from black felt. Cut the tongue from pink felt. Glue as shown.

4 Glue the black beads for eyes. Use the ribbon to make a shoestring bow (see page 141) with ½" loops and ½" tails. Glue at the back of the neck. For the hanger, thread the needle with nylon line, take a stitch under the bow, knot the ends and trim.

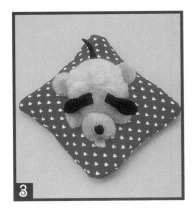

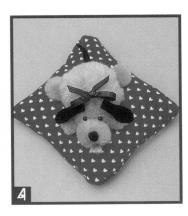

ear

tail

tongue

actual height 3"

actual height 3¾"

Shell Fairy & Pine Cone Angel

by Heather Foster

one 2½" wide white scallop shell
1⅛" wide starfish
one 1" wide wooden button
small handful of Spanish moss
round wooden toothpick
12" of gold thread
3" of 4mm cream fused pearls
low temperature glue gun and sticks or tacky craft glue

by Nancy Overmyer

one 2" long pine cone
one 1" round wooden bead
black fine-tip permanent pen
two 1⅞" long green silk ivy leaves
6" of nylon monofilament fishing line
6" sprig of green artificial mini pine
six ¼" round red artificial berries
small handful of Spanish moss
low temperature glue gun and sticks or tacky craft glue

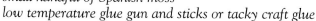

1 Cut 6" of thread and knot the ends together. Glue to the back of the button, then glue to the shell as shown in the photo at left.

2 Cut the toothpick to 2". Cut the remaining thread in half and tie each half around the cut end of the toothpick. Glue the starfish over the knots as shown in the large photo above.

3 Glue the moss for hair. Form the pearls into a circle and glue for her halo.

1 Transfer (see page 143) the face pattern to the bead and go over the lines with the pen. Glue the bead to the cone.

2 Knot the ends of the nylon line together and glue the knot to the upper back of the cone. Glue the ivy leaves over the knot for wings. Glue moss for hair. Shape the pine into a 1½" circle and glue for a halo. Glue the berries evenly spaced around the halo.

Christmas Seal

by Suzanne Jones

1" round wrapped peppermint candy
white pom poms:
*   three 1", two 5mm*
black half-round beads: two 3mm, one 4mm
3" square of white felt
½" square of green felt
3 red seed beads
12" of nylon fishing line
needle
tracing paper, pencil
low temperature glue gun and sticks or tacky
*   craft glue*

actual length 2½"

flippers

tail

holly leaf

1 Body: For the center, trim opposite sides of a 1" pom pom flat. Trim one side of each remaining 1" pom pom flat and glue these on each side of the center.

2 Trim the tail pom poms, tapering them to a point. Trace the patterns. Cut two flippers and a tail from white felt. Glue the tail as shown.

3 Glue the bottom center of the body to the mint, with the cellophane "tails" extending to the sides. Glue the straight edge of one flipper to the seal's side, curve the flipper downward and glue the rounded end to the candy. Repeat on the other side. Glue the 5mm pom poms side by side on the front of the head for his muzzle. Cut four 1" lengths of nylon line and glue two on each side for whiskers.

4 Glue the 4mm bead for a nose and the 3mm beads for eyes. Cut two holly leaves from green felt. Glue to the back of the neck as shown. Glue the seed beads in a triangle for berries. Thread the remaining nylon line on the needle and take a stitch through the neck. Knot the line ends together to make a hanger.

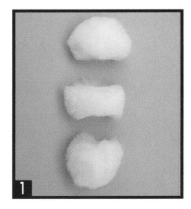

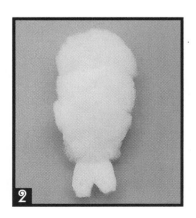

Bell Angel

by Loyal Hjelmervik

1 ¼" wide gold jingle bell
one ⅞" round wooden bead with a ⅛" hole
10" of 2" wide white double-layered gathered lace
9" of 1 ¼" wide gold mesh ribbon
5" of blonde Mini Curl™ curly hair
one ¾" wide gold wedding ring
12" of ⅛" wide cream satin ribbon
12" of nylon monofilament fishing line
30-gauge wire
acrylic paints: light peach, black, pink
paintbrushes: #00 liner, #4 flat
pink powdered blush, cotton swab
needle, cream thread
low temperature glue gun and sticks or tacky craft glue

actual height 3"

1 Tie the fishing line to the top of the bell for a hanger. Sew a running stitch along the bound edge of the lace and gather tightly; glue to the top of the bell.

2 Paint the bead peach; let dry. Transfer (see page 143) the face pattern to the front of the bead. Dip the handle of the liner in pink paint and touch to the mouth three times to dot the lips. Dip it in black paint to dot the eyes. Use the liner to paint the eyebrows, eyelashes and nostrils. Blush her cheeks. Thread the hanger through the hole in the bead, slide the bead down and glue to the top of the ball. Cut the hair into 1" lengths and rub between your fingers to frizz it. Glue the hair and halo as shown.

back view

3 Fold the mesh ribbon ends to the center, overlapping them slightly, and wire to secure. Glue to her back for wings. Cut the cream ribbon in half and use each half to make a shoestring bow (see page 141) with ½" loops and ½" tails. Glue one to the center of the wings and the other under her chin.

Puffy Velour Heart

by Cynthia Sullivan

4"x8" piece of lightweight cardboard
5"x10" piece of burgundy velour fabric
8" square of polyester batting
12" of 6mm cream fused pearls
⅞ yard of 3mm cream fused pearls
5" of 4" long cream satin fringe
1½ yards of 1/16" wide mauve satin ribbon
tracing paper, pencil
low temperature glue gun and sticks or tacky craft glue

actual length 7" including fringe

1 Trace the heart pattern and cut two from cardboard. Lay the hearts on the batting and cut four batting hearts slightly larger than the cardboard ones. Cut the velour into two 5" squares. Lay a velour square right side down on the table. Center two batting hearts on it, then a cardboard heart on top. Pull the velour over the cardboard edges, gluing as you go; clip the velour as needed to form smooth curves. Let the glue set, then trim excess fabric. Repeat for a second heart.

2 Glue fringe to the bottom center back of one heart. Cut a 6" ribbon length, knot the ends and glue the knot at the center top as shown.

3 Glue the hearts together, right sides out. Glue 6mm pearls to cover the seam.

4 Cut a 10" ribbon length and set aside. Hold the remaining ribbon and 3mm pearls together to make a loopy bow (see page 140) with six 1" loops and 3" tails. Tie the center with the 10" length. Glue the bow to the center top of the heart.

Potpourri Umbrella

by Cynthia Sullivan

9" of 18-gauge wire
white floral tape
20-gauge white cloth-covered wire
5"x10" piece of mauve satin fabric
⅜ yard of 1½" wide cream gathered lace
6" of ⅛" wide cream satin ribbon
⅝ yard of 3mm cream fused pearls
6" of cream marabou feathers
one 1" long dark pink silk rosebud
½ cup of potpourri
tracing paper, pencil
low temperature glue gun and sticks or tacky craft glue

actual length 7"

1 Wrap the wire spiral-fashion with the floral tape, completely covering it; repeat. Curve one end as shown. Trace the half-circle pattern and cut one from the satin fabric. Glue lace around the curved edge.

2 Fold the satin in half, right sides together, and glue along the straight edges to form a cone, leaving ¼" open at the point. Turn right side out. Insert the handle to extend ½" out the point. Fill the umbrella with potpourri. Wrap ribbon tightly around it 1" below the lace edge, knot and trim the ends.

3 Cut a ½" piece of marabou and glue to the tip. Glue the upper curved edges of the fabric together, then glue the remaining marabou along the bound edge of the lace.

4 Use the pearls to make a loopy bow (see page 140) with eight 1" loops and 2½" tails. Glue to the ribbon; glue the rosebud in the bow center.

Potpourri Angel

by Suzanne Jones

1¼" round wooden ball
½" round wooden bead
¼ yard of 3½" wide cream flat lace with 2 scalloped edges
⅛ cup of potpourri
3"x5¼" piece of cream tulle
18" of ¼" wide mauve satin ribbon
three 1"–1½" sprigs of dried lavender
acrylic paints: light peach, white, pink
¼" flat paintbrush, round wooden toothpick
black fine-tip permanent pen
pink powdered blush, cotton swab
handful of blonde Mini-Curl™ curly hair
6" of gold cord, 6" of 30-gauge wire
sewing machine or needle, cream thread
tracing paper, transfer paper, pencil
low temperature glue gun and sticks or tacky craft glue

actual height 5"

1 Dress: Cut a 5¼" length of lace. Place the tulle on the wrong side of the lace and handle as one. Fold in half crosswise and sew a ¼" seam along the 3½" edge. Turn right side out and stitch across the bottom, ½" from the edge. Sew a running stitch around the top edge. Fill with potpourri and pull the stitches to gather tightly; knot to secure.

2 Head and hands: Paint the wooden ball and bead peach; let dry. Transfer (see page 143) the face pattern. Draw the eyes, eyebrows, eyelashes, nostrils and mouth with the pen. Dip the paintbrush handle in pink paint and touch three times to the mouth to dot the lips. Dip the toothpick in white and dot the eye highlights. Blush the cheeks. Dip the paintbrush handle in white to dot the cheek highlights. Glue the head to the dress top. Glue the bead as shown for hands, turning it so the hole angles upward to the right (see the lavender in the large photo).

3 Hair: Cut into 3" lengths. Hold 3–4 lengths together and rub between your fingers to frizz. Glue the centers to the top front of the head. Repeat from front to back to cover the entire head.
Wings: Gather the remaining lace lengthwise and wire the center. Glue to her back.

4 Cut the ribbon into three equal lengths and use each to make a shoestring bow (see page 141) with ¾" loops and ¾" tails. Glue one to the wings as shown, one at her chin and one to the top of her hair as shown in the large photo. Glue the lavender into the hole of the hands. To make a hanger, knot the ends of the gold cord together and glue the knot to the back of her head.

back view

back view

actual width 5"

Carousel Horse

by Nancy Overmyer

dough (see page 142): white, blue, pink
1 black seed bead
acrylic paints: peach, brown, white, blue
paintbrushes: #4 flat, #00 liner
9" of ⅛" wide wooden dowel
1½" of 30-gauge wire
round toothpick, knife
foil-lined cookie sheet
polymer sealer (such as EnviroTex® Lite or
Ultra-Glo)

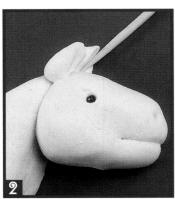

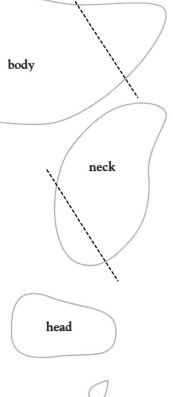

body

neck

head

ear

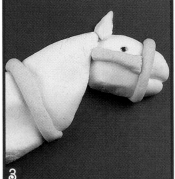

1 (Use white dough unless otherwise instruct-
ed.) **Body:** Form a 1¼" ball into a teardrop
shape. Flatten slightly and turn the tip upward to
match the pattern. Cut off the tip at the dashed
line. Use your thumb to press indentations into
the shoulders and hips. **Neck:** Roll a 1" ball into a
teardrop, curve the tip forward and cut the round end
as shown. Moisten the cut surface with water and attach
to the cut surface of the body.

2 **Head:** Roll a ¾" ball into a pear shape. Use the knife to
cut the mouth. Indent the nostrils with a toothpick.
Press the black bead in for the eye. Moisten with water and
attach to the front of the neck. **For each ear:** Shape a ⅜"
ball into a teardrop. Moisten with water and attach to the
back of the head, then indent the front lengthwise with a
toothpick.

3 **Harness:** Roll a ½" pink ball into a ⅛" thick rope. Cut
a ½" length and attach to the side of the head below
the eye. Cut a 1¼" length and and wrap it over the nose.
Wrap the rest over the neck seam as shown; cut off excess.

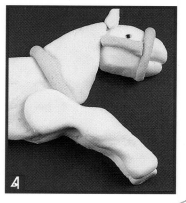

4 **For each foreleg:** Roll a ¾" ball into a log, then roll to thin the legs, leaving bulges for the knee, shoulder and hoof. Pinch to shape the hoof; flatten the shoulder. Attach as shown.

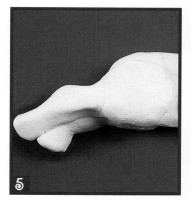

foreleg

hind leg

5 **For each back leg:** Begin with a 1" ball and shape as for the front leg, but position the indentations farther down, leaving a larger hip. Make the hip on the back side of the ornament smaller and flatter to reduce bulk and allow it to lie flat.

6 **Saddle:** Flatten a ½" ball of pink dough into an oval and attach to the back. Pinch a ¼" ball of blue into a stirrup, indent with the knife tip and attach just below the saddle. Roll a ⅛"x2" pink rope and attach around the rump behind the saddle. Repeat for a blue rope below the pink one.

saddle

stirrup

7 **Mane and forelock:** Roll three ⅜" balls of blue dough into a long, tapered teardrops. Attach the rounded ends to the top of the neck. Use a toothpick to make a lengthwise indentation in the center of each, then curve the tip forward and up for a flowing appearance. Repeat for the forelock, but use a ¼" ball.

mane

forelock

8 **Tail:** Shape a 1" blue ball into a teardrop. Flatten the small end slightly and curve it under (see arrow). Cut the rounded end flat. Indent hair lines with the knife, then attach to the rump as shown.

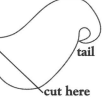

tail

cut here

9 Wrap the wire around the dowel and twist the ends together to make a hanger; remove. Insert the dowel through the center of the saddle and out through the belly of the horse, twisting it and applying gentle pressure. Insert the twisted ends of the hanger behind the dowel. Bake at 325° until hard.

Refer to the large photo on page 126 for painting. Paint the pole blue; let dry, then add diagonal stripes of white. Thin brown paint with an equal amount of water and paint the hooves. Thin peach paint with an equal amount of water to blush the nose and inner ears. Allow to dry, then seal (see page 142).

Cinnamon Reindeer

by Carol Rice & Marion Lewis

four 3" long cinnamon sticks
5"x6" piece of brown felt
12" long brown chenille stem
3" square of green felt
3"x12" strip of red/green Christmas print fabric
6" of 1/16" wide red satin ribbon
12" of gold thread
brown pom poms: one 1 1/2", one 3/4"
one 1/4" red pom pom
two 10mm wiggle eyes
two 6mm gold beads
sewing machine or needle, red and brown thread
long darning needle or soft-sculpture needle
polyester fiberfill
tracing paper
pencil
low temperature glue gun and sticks or tacky craft glue

arm placement

body

ear

leg placement

actual height 9"

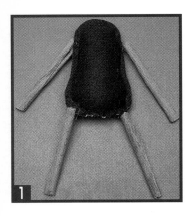

1 Trace the patterns. Cut two ears and two body pieces from brown felt. Set the ears aside for step 4. Glue the body pieces together with a 1/8" seam, leaving 1" open at the bottom. Stuff firmly; glue the opening closed. To attach each leg and arm, thread a long needle with brown thread and knot the thread ends together. Take a stitch at one placement dot on the body, then insert the needle through one side of a cinnamon stick. Bring it up through the other side and take another stitch through the body. Knot and cut the thread.

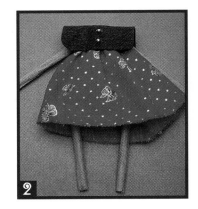

2 **Dress:** Sew a running stitch 1/4" from one long edge of the fabric and pull to gather under the arms. Overlap the back edges 1/2" and glue. Trim to round the edges of the green felt square, center it over the dress top and glue in place. Glue the gold beads for buttons.

3 **Head:** Glue the 1 1/2" pom pom to the dress top, the 3/4" pom pom for a muzzle and the red pom pom for a nose. Glue on the eyes. Use the ribbon to make a shoestring bow (see page 141) with 1/2" loops and 1/2" tails; glue above one eye.

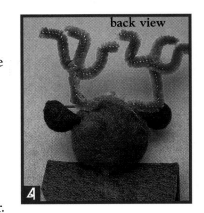

back view

4 **Ears:** Fold each in half lengthwise and glue the bottom edges together. Glue 1" apart to the head as shown. **Antlers:** Cut the chenille stem into four 3" lengths. Twist one around another 1" from the top, then bend as shown. Glue behind one ear. Repeat, bending the second opposite to the first. For a hanger, thread a needle with gold thread and sew through the top back dress yoke. Knot the thread ends together.

Paper Twist Elf

by Nancy Overmyer

4" wide twisted paper ribbon:
18" of blue-green, 11" of white
one 1 ½" wide Styrofoam® ball
2¼ of 1⅜" wide red plaid ribbon
6" of ¼" wide red satin ribbon
two 6mm black half-round beads
acrylic paints: orange, black
#00 liner paintbrush
round wooden toothpick
20-gauge wire, wire cutters
pink powdered blush, cotton swab
tracing paper, pencil
low temperature glue gun and sticks or
   tacky craft glue

1 Head: Untwist the white paper ribbon. Cut a 10" length and place the foam ball 2" from one end. Wrap the ribbon around it; glue the edges together. Twist both ends tightly close to the ball; wire to secure. Cut the paper ribbon in half from the center bottom almost to the neck and spread apart for arms.

2 Body: Untwist the blue-green paper ribbon. Cut off 3" and set aside for step 3. Fold the remainder in half crosswise. Gather ½" from the ends, forming a ruffle, and insert the arms through the ruffle. Push the ruffle close to the head and wire tightly just below it. Cut one end of the plaid ribbon to a point and the other in an inverted V. Glue for his bib. Glue the beads for buttons. Use the satin ribbon to make a shoestring bow (see page 141) with ½" loops and ½" tails. Glue at his neck. Bring the ends of the arms to the front and twist together 1" from the ends.

bib

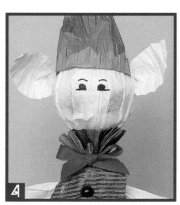

actual height 10"

3 Hat: Cut one 4" edge of the remaining blue-green ribbon in a zig-zag. Fold this edge up ½". Overlap and glue the 3" edges together to form a tube, then pinch and twist the top, gluing to secure. Glue the hat to the top of his head.

4 Ears: Trace the ear pattern. From the remaining white ribbon, cut two ears. Pinch the short straight edge of one and glue to the side of his head with the longer straight edge at the top and the curved edge at the bottom. Repeat on the other side. Transfer (see page 143) the face pattern. Paint the eyes and eyebrows black. Paint the nose, mouth and freckles orange. Blush the cheeks.

ear

actual height 7"

Ragged Rabbit

by Dawn Quick

Note: tear all straight fabric edges, rather than cutting them, to create the ragged look.

red/cream striped calico fabric: 7"x4½" piece, 9½"x4½" piece
Christmas print fabric with tan background: five 4"x½" strips, 16½"x3" strip
unbleached muslin fabric: 4½" circle, 1½"x5" strip
polyester fiberfill
black fine-tip permanent pen
pink powdered blush, cotton swab
needle, tan thread
tracing paper, pencil
low temperature glue gun and sticks or tacky craft glue

4½" circle

1 Legs and arms: On each striped fabric piece, turn under ¼" of each long edge, then fold in half lengthwise, wrong sides together. Tie each striped piece 1" from each end with a 4" print strip. Wrap the center of each piece tightly with thread and knot to secure. Fold the longer leg piece in half and glue for 1" below the thread.

2 Dress: Sew a running stitch along one long edge of the 16½"x3" print fabric. Pull to gather the fabric tightly; knot to secure. Overlap and glue the 3" ends together in the back. Glue the center of the arms to the dress top. Glue the legs inside the dress as high as they will go.

3 Head: Lay the muslin circle over the face pattern, centering the face near the top of the lower half. Trace the features with the pen. Blush the cheeks. Sew a running stitch ¾" inside the circle edge and pull to gather it into a pouch. Stuff softly with fiberfill, gather tightly and knot to secure. Glue the head over the center of the arms. Knot the remaining 4" print strip in the center and glue the knot below her chin.

4 Ears: Trace the pattern on the fold of tracing paper. Open and cut two ear pieces from muslin. Sew together with long running stitches ⅛" from the outer edge. Wrap thread tightly around the center and knot to secure. Glue the center to the top of her head. For a hanger, take a stitch through the head behind the ears. Cut the thread ends to 4" and knot the ends together.

fold line

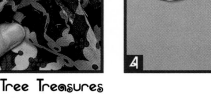

ears

Bunny on a Sled

by Teresa Nelson

one 2½"x4" red miniature sled
two 1½"tan pom poms
four 1"tan pom poms
one ¾" tan pom pom
two ½" white pom poms
one 5mm pink pom pom
two 5mm black half-round beads
2½"x4" piece of tan felt
1½"x2½" piece of pink felt
6" of ¼" wide green satin ribbon
18" of gold metallic thread
tracing paper, pencil
low temperature glue gun and sticks or
    tacky craft glue

actual height 4"

1 Glue the two 1½" pom poms together for the body. Glue the body to the sled.

2 Glue the 1" pom poms for feet and hands. Glue the ¾" pom pom for a tail.

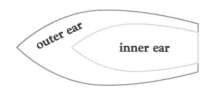

outer ear

inner ear

3 Glue the white pom poms side by side for a muzzle. Glue the pink pom pom above the white ones for a nose. Glue the beads for eyes. **Ears:** Trace the patterns. Cut two tan outer ears and two pink inner ears. Glue together as shown on the pattern, then glue to the top of the bear's head.

4 Use the ribbon to make a shoestring bow (see page 141) with ¾" loops and ¾" tails. Glue to the neck. For a hanger, knot one end of the gold thread to each side of the sled front. Find the center point of the thread and glue it under the center back of the sled.

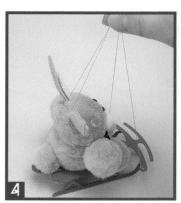

actual height 3"

Geek Love

by Sandy Zimmer

dough (see page 142): red, white, natural, pink,
   green, brown, gray
7" of ⅜" wide gray grosgrain ribbon
black fine-tip permanent pen
acrylic paints: blue, red
#2 round paintbrush
foil-lined cookie sheet
matte acrylic sealer (such as DecoArt™
   Americana™ Sealer/Finisher spray or Delta
   Ceramcoat® brush-on matte sealer)
polymer sealer (such as EnviroTex® Lite or
   Ultra-Glo)
1½" of 30-gauge wire

hair

hand

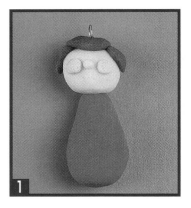

1 **Boy:** Roll a 1" red dough ball into a 1½" long teardrop. Attach a ¾" natural ball to the pointed end for a head. Roll a 1/16" natural ball and attach to the center of the head for the nose. Slightly flatten two ⅛" pink balls and attach one on each side of the nose for cheeks. Roll three ¼" balls into teardrops, flatten and attach for his hair—place the first two point to point, draping down the sides of his head, then place the third over the points at an angle with the round end extending forward. Wrap the wire around the paintbrush handle and twist the ends to make a hanger; insert into the top of his head.

2 **Computer:** Flatten a ½" gray ball into a 1"x¾" rectangle. Roll a ¼"x4" white rope and wrap it around the gray, joining and smoothing the ends. For the keyboard, shape a ¾" white dough ball into a 1½"x⅝" parallelogram and attach at the bottom. Join to the boy's body as shown.

arm

3 **Arms:** Roll two ¾" red balls into 1⅜" logs with slightly thinner centers. Attach one extending over the top of the computer screen. Bend the other arm and attach to his side as shown.

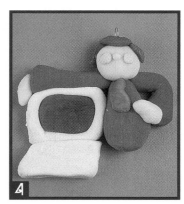

4 Pinch two ⅜" natural balls into teardrops and attach the blunt ends to the arms—curve his right hand lovingly around the computer screen. Roll a ½" green ball into a ¾" long teardrop and attach for his tie. Bake at 315° until hard; let cool. Referring to the patterns and the large photo, paint blue stripes on his tie and a red heart on the computer. Apply matte sealer and let dry, then use the pen to draw his eyes, mouth, the computer keys, and "I…MY COMPUTER" on the screen. Recoat with matte sealer, let dry, and seal with polymer sealer (see page 142). Insert the ribbon through the hanger and glue the ends together.

An Apple for the Teacher

by Sandy Zimmer

dough (see page 142): red, white, natural, pink, green, blue, brown, black
2" square blackboard
½" tall red apple with leaf
7" of ⅜" wide blue grosgrain ribbon
black fine-tip permanent pen
garlic press
matte acrylic sealer (such as DecoArt™ Americana™ Sealer/Finisher spray or Delta Ceramcoat® brush-on matte sealer)
polymer sealer (such as EnviroTex® Lite or Ultra-Glo)
low temperature glue gun and sticks or tacky craft glue
1 ½" of 30-gauge wire
foil-lined cookie sheet

holly

actual height 4"

1 Body: Roll a ¾" ball of red dough into a 1" long teardrop. Roll a ¾" ball of blue dough into a ¾" long teardrop. Moisten the top of the blue teardrop and attach to the blunt end of the red one. Roll two ¼"x¾" natural logs. Attach side by side for legs. Press the teacher against the side of the blackboard.

2 Head: (Pattern on page 132.) Attach a ¾" natural ball to the red pointed end. Roll a ¹⁄₁₆" natural ball and attach to the center of the head for the nose. Slightly flatten two ⅛" pink balls and attach one on each side of the nose for cheeks. Press brown dough through the garlic press and use a toothpick to slide off ¼" lengths for her hair. Wrap the wire around the paintbrush handle and twist the ends to make a hanger; insert into the top of her head.

3 Arms: (Patterns on page 132.) Roll two ¾" red balls into 1⅜" logs with slightly thinner centers. Attach one extending over the top of the blackboard. Bend the other arm and attach to her side as shown. **Hands:** Pinch two ⅜" natural balls into teardrops; attach the rounded ends as shown.

4 Feet: Shape two ½" black balls into teardrops and attach with the rounded ends at the sides. **Holly:** Roll three ⅜" long green teardrops and attach in a triangle as shown, points outward. Roll three ⅛" red balls and attach for the berries. Bake at 325° until hard; let cool. Apply matte sealer and let dry, then use the pen to draw the eyes and mouth. Recoat with matte sealer, let dry, and seal with polymer sealer (see page 142). Use the satin ribbon to make a shoestring bow (see page 141) with ½" loops and ½" tails; glue under her chin. Glue the apple into her raised hand. Insert the grosgrain ribbon through the hanger and glue the ends together.

Cinnamon Dough Ornaments

by Suzanne Jones

cinnamon dough:

2 cups of cinnamon
1½ cups of applesauce
mixing bowl and spoon
plastic bag

ornaments:

spatula
waxed paper, emery board
rolling pin
two 1"x9" strips of ¼" thick wood
round wooden toothpicks
*paper clips, wire cutters, ⅛" wide
    ribbon or cord (for hangers)*
assorted cookie cutters
*acrylic or dimensional paints,
    lace, ribbons, beads,
    flowers, sequins, etc.
    of your choice for
    decorating the ornaments*
*low temperature glue gun and
    sticks or tacky craft glue*

1 Mix the cinnamon with one cup of the applesauce. Continue adding applesauce a little at a time until the dough reaches a firm consistency. Store unused dough in a plastic bag.

2 Place the dough on waxed paper with a wood strip on each side as shown—place the strips just far enough apart so the ends of your rolling pin can rest on them. Cover the dough with another piece of waxed paper and roll to ¼" thick. Remove the top waxed paper.

3 Cut out shapes with cookie cutters. For hangers, use a toothpick to make a small hole in the top of each ornament, or cut paper clips in half and insert into the tops.

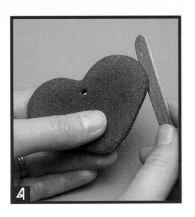

4 With the spatula, transfer the ornaments to a flat area where they can dry away from direct heat. Turn them often; it will take about five days for them to dry completely. As they dry, they will become lighter in color. After drying, use an emery board to smooth the outer edges. Use the ideas below to decorate your ornaments, or create your own! Thread ribbon or cord through the hangers.

Lacy Heart Ornament:

Glue ¾" wide ivory gathered crocheted lace around the back of a cinnamon dough heart. Use ⅛" wide ivory satin ribbon for the hanger, then use the same ribbon to make a shoestring bow (see page 141). Glue a ribbon rose to the bow center, then glue the bow over the base of the hanger.

Gingerbread Boy:

Squeeze dots of dimensional paint for eyes and buttons on a cinnamon dough figure, then use a liner paintbrush to squiggle acrylic "frosting" around the edges. Use different cookie cutter sizes to make a whole family!

For a Special Teacher:

Use acrylic or dimensional paint to write your own message on a cinnamon dough apple. Add a shoestring bow and hanger of bright red satin ribbon.

Hearts & Stars Wall Hanging:

An extra-large cinnamon dough heart is the base for this plaque. The "stitches" were painted with a liner brush and red acrylic paint. A 12" raffia length, knotted through holes in both shoulders of the heart, makes a hanger. The glued-on cinnamon dough stars were embellished with blue or green stitches and assorted buttons.

actual width 4¾"

Baby's 1st Christmas

by Marilyn Gossett

4¾" circle of 140# watercolor paper
one 3½" wide clear acrylic rocking horse
   (this ornament uses half)
15" of 6mm gold fused beads
one ⅜" wide pink ribbon rose
12" of ⅛" wide dusty rose satin ribbon
one 1½" long blue diaper pin
one 1¼" long white/pink baby rattle
one 1⅛" long white/blue baby bottle
acrylic paints: yellow, blue, pink
paintbrushes: #0 round, ½" flat
black fine-tip permanent pen
tracing paper, transfer paper, pencil
low temperature glue gun and sticks or tacky
   craft glue

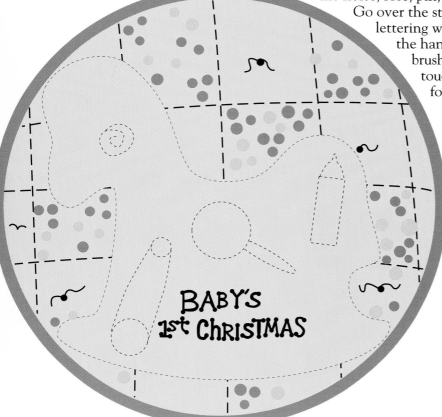

1 Paint the circle yellow. Dilute blue paint with an equal amount of water to paint the border. Transfer (see page 143) the lettering and stitching patterns (do not transfer the fine dashed placement lines for the horse, rose, pin, rattle and bottle). Go over the stitching lines and lettering with the pen. Dip the handle of the round brush in blue paint and touch to make the blue dots; repeat with pink paint for the pink dots.

2 Glue the rose, pin, rattle and bottle in place. Cut the hanging loop off the horse and glue him in place; glue the beads around the horse. Use the ribbon to make a shoestring bow (see page 141) with ¾" loops and 1" tails. Glue to the center top as shown in the large photo. Glue the ends of the remaining ribbon to the back for a hanger.

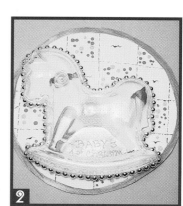

BABY'S
1st CHRISTMAS

1st Class Teacher

by Marilyn Gossett

5" square of 140# watercolor paper
one 1⅛" wide wood button
one 3" wide clear acrylic heart (this ornament uses half)
15" of 6mm gold fused beads
acrylic paints: light peach, black, white, mauve, orange, tan
pink powdered blush, cotton swab
5" of blonde Mini-Curl™ curly hair
4" of 28-gauge gold wire
12" of ⅛" wide red satin ribbon
1"x¾" scrap of white paper
round wooden toothpick, wire cutters
one ½" red artificial apple with leaf
paintbrushes: #0 round, ½" flat
black fine-tip permanent pen
red pen
tracing paper, transfer paper, pencil
low temperature glue gun and sticks or tacky craft glue

actual size 4¾"x5"

1 Paint the heart black. Transfer (see page 143) the stitching line and lettering; paint them white.

2 **Pencil:** Cut the toothpick to 1¼" long. Paint the point tan, the very tip black and the rest orange, to look like a pencil. Write a red "A+" on the paper. Glue the paper, pencil and apple in place. Glue the heart over them, then glue beads around it.

3 Refer to the large photo. Paint the button peach. Transfer the face pattern and go over the lines with the pen. Dip the round paintbrush handle in mauve paint and touch to the mouth to make three dots for lips. Blush the cheeks. Glue above the acrylic heart. Cut the hair into 1" lengths, glue as shown and fluff.

Form the remaining beads into a circle and glue for a halo. For glasses, curve the wire twice around the paintbrush handle (see diagram); glue to her face. Use the ribbon to make a shoestring bow with ½" loops and ¾" tails; glue at her chin. Glue the ends of the remaining ribbon to the top back for a hanger.

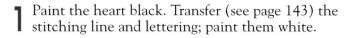

Dough Reindeer

by Nancy Overmyer

dough (see page 142): white, red, brown
6" of green satin ribbon
two 4mm black beads
polymer sealer (such as EnviroTex® Lite or Ultra-Glo)
acrylic paints: white, red
#00 liner paintbrush
X-acto® knife, foil-lined cookie sheet
1½" of 30-gauge wire
6" of gold cord
round wooden toothpick
low temperature glue gun and sticks or tacky craft glue

For a charming holiday pin, omit the hanger and glue on a ¾" pin back.

actual height 2"

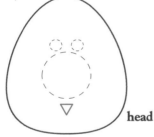

head

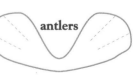

ears

1 Face: Roll a 1" brown ball into an egg and flatten slightly to match the head pattern. Roll a ½" red dough ball and attach for his nose. Use the paintbrush handle to indent a mouth below the nose. Press in the beads for eyes.

2 For each ear: Shape a ⅜" brown ball into a teardrop and use the toothpick to indent it lengthwise. Attach the ears to the head as shown, with the pointed ends ¼" apart.

3 Antlers: Roll a ⅝" white ball into a dumbbell. Pull the center down and pinch to a point, matching the pattern. Make two cuts in each antler, then smooth and round the antlers as shown. Attach to the center top of his head.
Forelock: Flatten a ¼" brown ball into a teardrop, attach with the point over the center of the antlers and imprint hair lines with the toothpick. Curve the wire around a pencil to form a hanging loop; twist the ends together and insert behind his antlers. Bake at 325° until hard; let cool. Paint white highlights on his nose and eyes as shown in the large photo above. Paint the mouth red. Seal (see page 142). Use the ribbon to make a shoestring bow (see page 141) and glue it to the side of his chin. Insert the gold cord through the hanger and knot the ends together.

antlers

forelock